ITALIAN COMFORT FOOD

Also by the Scotto Family

FRESCO: MODERN TUSCAN COOKING FOR ALL SEASONS

ROME, 1932.

ITALIAN COMFORT FOOD

Intensive Eating from

FRESCO *by Scotto* RESTAURANT

Marion Scotto

Rosanna Scotto

Anthony Scotto Jr.

Elaina Scotto

ReganBooks
Celebrating Ten Bestselling Years
An Imprint of HarperCollins*Publishers*

WE DEDICATE THIS COOKBOOK TO OUR FUTURE GENERATION:

Jenna, L.J., Anthony III, Dan Jr., Gabriella, Julia, and Bianca

A hardcover edition of this book was published in 2002 by ReganBooks, an imprint of HarperCollins Publishers.

FIRST PAPERBACK EDITION PUBLISHED 2005.

Professional photographs by Sacha Frey, except for the dedication-page photograph by Nina Drapaez
All other photographs courtesy of the authors

The Library of Congress has cataloged the hardcover edition as follows:

Italian comfort food : intensive eating from Fresco by Scotto Restaurant / Marion Scotto...[et al.].—1st ed.
p. cm.
ISBN 0-06-051569-4
1. Cookery, Italian. 2. Fresco by Scotto (Restaurant) I. Scotto, Marion.

TX723.I793 2002
641.5945—dc21 2002069776

ISBN 0-06-051570-8 (pbk.)

05 06 07 08 09 IM 10 9 8 7 6 5 4 3 2 1

ACKNOWLEDGMENTS

A SPECIAL THANK-YOU TO OUR COLLEAGUES
FOR THEIR KINDNESS AND SUPPORT THROUGHOUT THE YEARS:

Cindy Adams
Arthur and Trish Backal
Michael Bass
Katie Couric
Ann Curry
Gillian Duffy
Florence Fabricant
Kathie Lee Gifford
Rudolph Giuliani
Neil Goldstein
Gael Greene
Lisa Gregorich-Dempsey
Joan Hamburg
Richard Johnson
Alan Katz
Bob Lape
Matt Lauer
Esther Newberg
Rosie O'Donnell
Tony Potts
Regis Philbin
Robin Raisfeld
Judith Regan
Ruth Reichl
Al Roker
Hal Rubenstein
George Steinbrenner
Scott Sassa
Phil Suarez
Jonathan Tisch
Jonathan Wald
Bernie Young
Nina and Tim Zagat
Jeff Zucker

FRESCO

*A SPECIAL THANK-YOU TO THE FRESCO STAFF:

To *Stefano Battistini,* our executive chef, who has been with us since December 1997: Thank you for all of your creativity, great style of cooking, and delectable dishes, and for keeping us one of the finest Tuscan restaurants in New York City.

To *Chris Smreker,* our pastry chef, who has been with us since November 1996: Thank you for your over-the-top desserts, endless energy, and consistent originality.

To *Raul Ramirez, Carl Murphy,* and *Elpidio Escamilla:* Thank you for your hard work, diligence, and good spirit.

To our management team, *Attilio Vosilla, George Incata, Alex Curta, Johanna Madoff,* and *James Rotunno:* Thank you for your support, hard work, and loyalty.

To *Natasha Gelman,* our bookkeeper, who has been with us since day one: Thank you for your commitment and perfection.

To *Dennis Ryan,* who has been with us since the day we opened: Thank you for your endless hours on the computer and your dedication to our customers.

To the rest of our staff: Thank you for your enthusiasm, loyalty, and perseverance.

and...

To our loyal customers:

We're all family at Fresco, and we couldn't have done it without you!

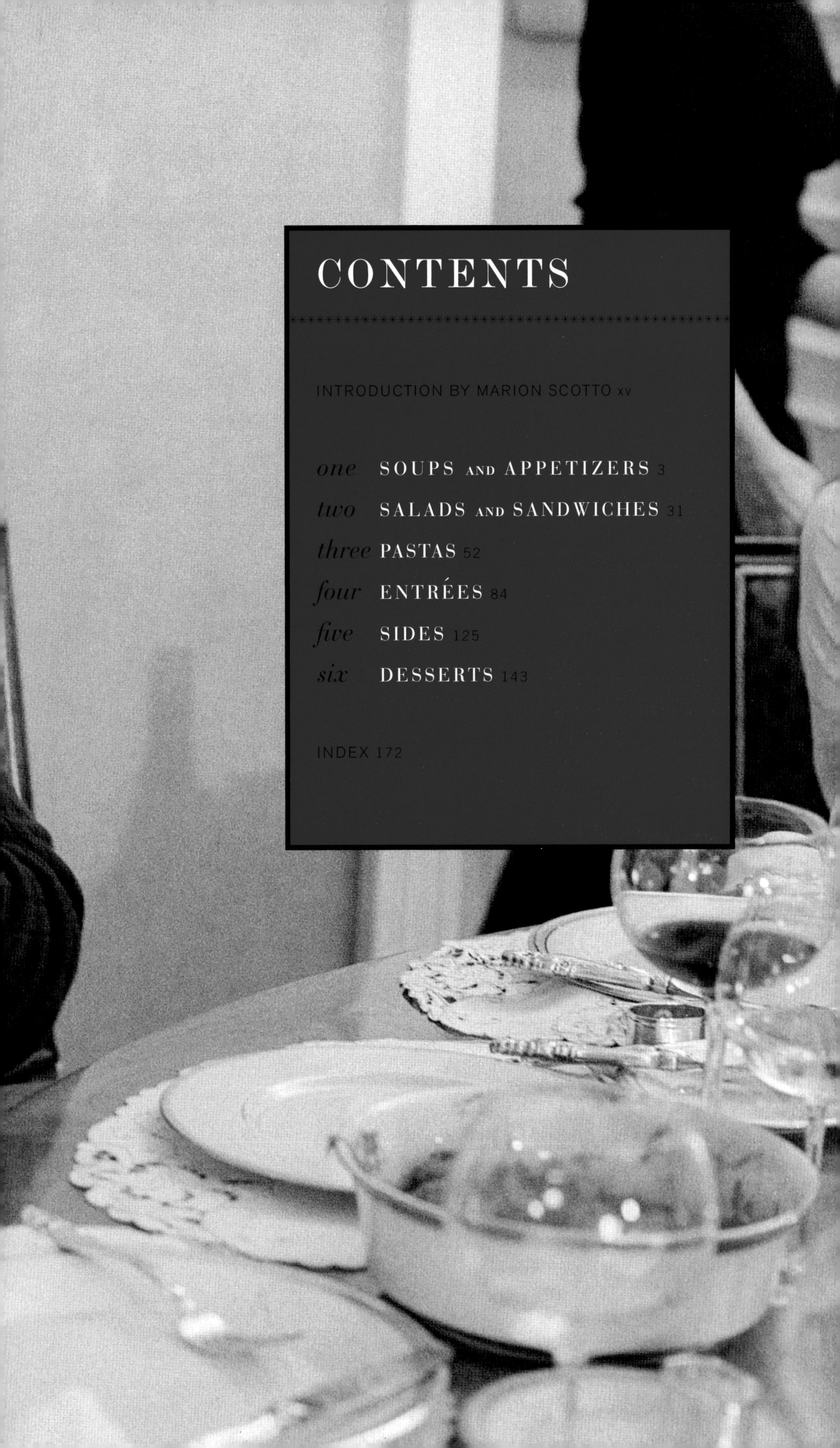

CONTENTS

Food has always been a focal point in our family's life. Some people eat to live, but we live to eat!

Our love of food began with my family in Brooklyn, in 1915. My grandparents owned a poultry market. While it was unusual for women to work outside the home in those days, my grandmother was an important part of the business. Her day was not over until she came home to cook and care for her six kids.

My mother eventually took over the business. She worked long hours and tried to make the best of what were difficult times during World War II. Food rationing was the way of life. So my mother cooked chicken in every way imaginable. I loved to watch her make boneless stuffed chicken; she deboned the chicken breast, stuffed it with mozzarella, sausage, and rice, and roasted it to a golden brown. It was better than roast beef.

I still use her recipes today, at home and at Fresco. There is something very comforting about cooking these dishes steeped in tradition.

Before we opened Fresco by Scotto restaurant in 1993, I did a lot of entertaining at home. As my children grew older, they refused to eat at the children's table. They wanted to sit with the adults. So I bought a big mahogany table that sat twenty people for serious eating.

I became so attached to this table that when we moved from Brooklyn into a Manhattan apartment, I took it with me . . . no easy task! We had to knock down a few walls, but it was worth it.

These days most of my entertaining at home is just for the immediate family—at last count seventeen people, including my seven wonderful grandchildren. My family's love of food has brought my children and grandchildren together. If we're not at Fresco, on a typical day you will find us in the kitchen, cooking and laughing.

Every summer, our family travels to Europe for intensive eating. We love to experience different foods from different countries. We bring these recipes back home and add the Fresco touch to them, so that our customers can enjoy them as much as we do.

Most of the recipes are simple, but you will find that the flavors are robust. We hope that you will have as much pleasure in preparing and eating these recipes as we have had over the years. —*Marion Scotto*

The poultry market, 1915.

Fresco Specialties

ITALIAN WEDDING SOUP

GRILLED PIZZA MARGHERITA

HOT PRESSED SOFT-SHELL CRAB CIABATTINI SANDWICH AND MEATBALL SANDWICH

FRESCO TIMPANO

RISOTTO WITH LOBSTER, SHRIMP, AND CALAMARI

MEATBALL LASAGNA

SPAGHETTI WITH LOBSTER AND SHRIMP RAGU

SUNDAY SAUCE WITH MEATBALLS, SAUSAGES, AND PORK CHOPS

CRESPELLE WITH SIX CHEESES

ZUPPA DI PESCE

GRANDMA'S BONELESS STUFFED CHICKEN

BRAISED LAMB SHANKS WITH ORANGE GREMOLATA

POTATO AND ZUCCHINI CHIPS

ORANGE BUNDT CAKE

PRALINE COOKIE ICE CREAM SANDWICHES AND SGROPPINO FLOAT

FRESCO STRAWBERRY SHORTCAKE
AND RASPBERRY MASCARPONE TART

Fresco Recipes

one

SOUPS AND APPETIZERS

SOUPS AND APPETIZERS ARE SUCH AN IMPORTANT PART OF THE MEAL, ESPECIALLY IF YOU'RE ENTERTAINING. AT HOME, WE NEVER START WITH JUST ONE APPETIZER. THERE'S ALWAYS SOMETHING THAT'S MADE FOR THE TABLE. WE LOVE TO HAVE OUR GUESTS AND FAMILY SHARE OUR WONDERFUL APPETIZERS.

CHILLED SUMMER MINESTRONE

4 TO 6 SERVINGS

We usually eat minestrone soup hot, but when visiting Florence we stumbled upon this tiny mom-and-pop restaurant where everyone sat at community tables. The mama in the kitchen chose everyone's menu. She made one appetizer and one entrée for the entire restaurant. Her special that day was chilled minestrone. We were pleasantly surprised to taste this cool soup on a very warm day, and it really hit the spot. It was one of the best meals we've ever had.

- 1 4-ounce piece fat of the PROSCIUTTO HAM
- 1 4-ounce rind PARMESAN CHEESE
- ½ cup OLIVE OIL
- 3 tablespoons chopped GARLIC
- 1 cup diced CARROTS
- 1 cup diced CELERY
- 1 cup diced ONION
- SALT and PEPPER
- Pinch of dried OREGANO
- ¼ cup TOMATO PASTE
- 2 quarts CHICKEN STOCK (see recipe on page 29)
- ½ cup BROCCOLI FLORETS
- ½ cup CAULIFLOWER FLORETS
- 2 cups cooked CANNELLINI BEANS
- ½ cup diced ZUCCHINI
- ½ cup uncooked TUBETTINI PASTA
- 6–8 thin slices PROSCIUTTO, cut into julienne strips
- 1 cup shaved PARMESAN CHEESE
- 1 cup diced PLUM TOMATOES
- 4–6 sprigs fresh BASIL

1. Place the prosciutto fat and the Parmesan cheese rind on a piece of cheesecloth. Make a "purse" by enclosing the bundle with a string. Set aside.

2. Heat the olive oil in a stockpot over medium heat. Add the garlic and sauté until it turns brown, about 1½ minutes. Add the carrots, celery, and onion and sauté until the onion is glazed, or about 4 minutes. Add salt and pepper to taste, the oregano, and the tomato paste.

3. Add the chicken stock and the cheesecloth sack. Bring to a boil over high heat, turn down the heat, and simmer for 20 minutes.

4. Add the broccoli, cauliflower, cannellini beans, and zucchini. Simmer for ½ hour, or until the vegetables are tender.

5. Add the pasta and cook for another 15 minutes, or until the pasta is al dente. At this point, the soup should have a nice, thick texture. Remove the cheesecloth and chill the soup in the refrigerator for 1 hour.

6. This soup can be served at room temperature or chilled. Garnish each bowl with julienned prosciutto, shaved Parmesan, diced tomatoes, and a sprig of fresh basil.

After September 11, 2001, New York was in shock. Business stopped, and people were glued to their TV sets. It seemed that time stood still.

One evening, just a few days after the attack, Mayor Rudolph Giuliani came in to have dinner. One of his favorite appetizers is our minestrone soup.

He looked around and said, "I never saw Fresco so empty." He grabbed my hand and said that he was determined to encourage people to return to a normal way of life. The mayor then said that he would support all businesses and would keep coming back until Fresco was busy again.

A few weeks later, the mayor returned, and Fresco was jam-packed with diners. As he entered the room, the entire restaurant stood up and applauded. It was one of the most touching moments in our lives. We are grateful to Mayor Giuliani for his love and support.

—Marion

We made this soup on the *Today* show for a segment called "What Christopher Columbus Ate on His Voyage to the New World." We took the liberty of tweaking a basic recipe that Christopher Columbus might have made so as to enhance the flavors. We also surprised Matt Lauer and Ann Curry that morning when Anthony actually dressed up as Christopher Columbus. It took all of their power to keep a straight face while they were interviewing us.

—*Marion and Elaina*

FIVE-BEAN SOUP

6 SERVINGS

½ cup uncooked CRANBERRY (BORLOTTI) BEANS

½ cup uncooked BLACK BEANS

½ cup uncooked RED BEANS

½ cup uncooked small WHITE (NAVY) BEANS (CANNELLINI OR TOSCANELLI)

½ cup BLACK-EYED PEAS

½ cup uncooked PEARL BARLEY

½ cup EXTRA-VIRGIN OLIVE OIL, plus additional for garnish

1 cup diced ONION

1 cup diced CARROTS

1 cup thinly sliced CELERY

1 tablespoon chopped GARLIC

1 tablespoon chopped fresh THYME

1 BAY LEAF

1 tablespoon chopped fresh SAGE

3 quarts CHICKEN STOCK (see recipe on page 29)

SEA SALT

Freshly ground BLACK PEPPER

1. Soak the beans separately in bowls of cold water overnight.

2. In a colander, combine the beans and the pearl barley. Rinse them thoroughly under cold running water. Drain the water off and set the mixture aside.

3. In a 6-quart heavy-bottomed stockpot, combine the olive oil, onion, carrots, celery, garlic, and herbs. Stir to coat the vegetables with the oil. Over moderate heat, cook the vegetables until they are fragrant and soft, or about 5 minutes.

4. Add the beans and pearl barley to the pot, stir them in to coat with oil, and cook for 1 minute more.

5. Add the chicken stock to the mixture and stir. Cover, bring to a gentle simmer over moderate heat, and cook until the outer shells of the largest beans are tender, or about 45 minutes.

6. Add salt to taste and cook until the beans are tender, or 15 to 45 minutes more. Stir occasionally to make sure the beans do not stick to the bottom of the stockpot. (Cooking time will vary according to the size and freshness of the beans.)

7. To serve, ladle the piping hot soup into warmed shallow soup bowls. Then drizzle extra-virgin olive oil directly into each bowl and add freshly ground pepper to taste. (This soup may be reheated several times over a period of 2 to 3 days. It will thicken. Simply thin the soup with water each time you reheat it.)

MARINATED SEAFOOD SALAD

6 SERVINGS

We make this traditional dish for Christmas Eve, and everyone loves it. It is somewhat time consuming, but you can prepare it at least a day in advance. The longer it marinates, the better it tastes. There's nothing like fresh seafood salad.

- 2 cups WHITE WINE
- 1½ tablespoons BLACK PEPPERCORNS
- 3 GARLIC CLOVES, whole
- 2 BAY LEAVES
- 3 quarts WATER
- Juice of 1 LEMON
- 2 pounds OCTOPUS (will shrink by half when cooked)
- 1 pound medium SHRIMP, peeled and deveined
- 1 pound CALAMARI, cleaned and cut into rings
- ½ cup julienned CARROTS
- ½ cup julienned ONIONS
- ½ cup julienned CELERY
- ½ cup EXTRA-VIRGIN OLIVE OIL, plus additional for garnish
- ½ cup chopped GARLIC
- ½ cup chopped fresh PARSLEY
- 1 cup ORANGE SEGMENTS
- 2 cups ORANGE JUICE
- SALT and PEPPER

1. In a large pot, combine the white wine, peppercorns, whole garlic cloves, bay leaves, water, and lemon juice. Bring to a boil, then lower the temperature to a simmer. Add the octopus and let it simmer for 45 minutes, or until tender. Remove from the heat and let the octopus cool in the liquid; this can be done 2 days in advance. Remove the octopus from the liquid, cover, and refrigerate.

2. Cook the shrimp and calamari in the same liquid for 3 minutes, and then let them cool in the liquid. Remove the shrimp and calamari, cover, and refrigerate.

3. Using the same water, parboil the carrots, onions, and celery for 1 minute. Drain and cool the vegetables.

4. Remove the soft purple skin and suckers from the octopus. Marinate it for 1 hour in a mixture of the olive oil, chopped garlic, and parsley.

5. On a hot grill, cook the octopus for 10 minutes, or until tender. Cut it into ¼-inch pieces.

6. Mix the seafood, vegetables, orange segments, and orange juice in a large bowl and marinate them for at least 12 hours before serving. Add salt, pepper, and olive oil to taste.

CROSTINI WITH PROSCIUTTO-ARTICHOKE DIP

6 SERVINGS

This is a great dish to make for a party. You can prepare it ahead of time, then just place it on your buffet table and leave the eating up to your guests.

FOR THE DIP

- 1½ cups SOUR CREAM
- ½ cup MAYONNAISE
- 6 ARTICHOKE HEARTS, sliced
- ½ pound PROSCIUTTO, thinly sliced and diced
- Juice of 1 LEMON
- 2 dashes TABASCO
- SALT and PEPPER

FOR THE CROSTINI

- 1 loaf ITALIAN BREAD (about 18 inches)
- 2 tablespoons chopped GARLIC
- ¼ cup EXTRA-VIRGIN OLIVE OIL
- ¼ cup chopped fresh OREGANO

1. Preheat the oven to 350°F.

2. *To make the dip:* In a large bowl, mix the sour cream, mayonnaise, artichoke hearts, and prosciutto.

3. Fold in the lemon juice, Tabasco, and salt and pepper to taste, and mix well. Set the dip aside.

4. *To make the crostini:* Cut the Italian bread into thin slices.

5. Brush the slices lightly with a mixture of the garlic and oil and season them with fresh oregano, and salt and pepper to taste.

6. Place the slices on a cookie sheet, and bake for 5 minutes, or until golden brown.

7. Serve the dip on a platter with the toasted bread crostini.

Overleaf: Marion's mother took this picture from the ship coming into New York from Italy in the 1940s. About twenty relatives showed up to meet them.

ARTICHOKE ALLA PARMIGIANA

6 SERVINGS

This is a great way to begin a meal or a special dinner.

One day Yankee boss George Steinbrenner, who is a loyal customer, especially during baseball season, was enjoying the Artichoke alla Parmigiana. George was emphasizing a point with his management team when he banged his hand on the table—and his diamond-encrusted World Series ring fell apart. There was a moment of silence and then suddenly George started laughing . . . and so did all of us. I knew there would be many more rings in his future! —Anthony

- 6 ARTICHOKES, sliced in half
- ½ cup OLIVE OIL
- Pinch of dried ROSEMARY
- Pinch of dried THYME
- Pinch of dried OREGANO
- 12 slices fresh MOZZARELLA
- SALT and PEPPER
- 4 EGG WHITES
- 1 cup ALL-PURPOSE FLOUR
- 2 cups TOMATO SAUCE (see recipe on page 79)
- 1 cup grated PARMESAN CHEESE
- ¼ cup chopped fresh BASIL

1. Cut the artichokes in half lengthwise. Combine them with a mixture of ¼ cup of the olive oil and the herbs. Cover and refrigerate for 1 to 3 hours.

2. Preheat the oven to 350°F. On a nonstick sheet pan, place the marinated artichoke halves cut-side up. Place 1 slice of mozzarella on top of each half. Add salt and pepper to taste.

3. In a metal bowl, beat the egg whites until fluffy.

4. In a sauté pan, heat the remaining ¼ cup olive oil over high heat and then lower to medium.

5. Dust the artichokes with the flour and dip them in the egg whites to cover. Place them in the sauté pan and cook for 1 minute on each side, or until golden brown. Drain them on paper towels and set aside.

6. Line the bottom of a casserole or baking dish with 1 cup of the tomato sauce. Layer all of the artichokes over the sauce. Line with another coat of tomato sauce and sprinkle with the Parmesan cheese. Bake in the oven, uncovered, for 5 to 7 minutes, or until the Parmesan cheese is melted. Sprinkle the artichokes with the chopped basil and serve hot.

ITALIAN WEDDING SOUP

6 SERVINGS

This traditional soup was served at weddings many years ago because it was satisfying and inexpensive to prepare. We still make it on cold days for our families. Cold water is the trick to making meatballs. If the mixture is moist, the meatballs will be tender and moist.

FOR THE MEATBALLS

- 1 pound ground BEEF
- 1 cup dried BREAD CRUMBS (store-bought are fine)
- 1 EGG
- 2 tablespoons chopped fresh PARSLEY
- ½ cup grated PARMESAN CHEESE
- 1 teaspoon KOSHER SALT
- Pinch of PEPPER
- 2 tablespoons cold WATER

FOR THE SOUP

- ½ cup OLIVE OIL
- 1 cup diced ONIONS
- 2 tablespoons chopped GARLIC
- 1 tablespoon crushed RED PEPPER FLAKES
- 2 quarts CHICKEN STOCK (see recipe on page 29)
- 1 cup diced CARROTS
- 1 cup diced CELERY
- ½ cup diced ZUCCHINI
- 1 pound ESCAROLE, chopped
- 5 tablespoons grated PARMESAN CHEESE
- SALT

1. *To make the meatballs:* Place the ground beef in a large bowl.

2. Add the bread crumbs, egg, parsley, cheese, salt, and pepper.

3. With wet, cold hands mix the ingredients together well.

4. Add the cold water. Form the mixture into about 18 one-inch meatballs. Set aside.

5. *To make the soup:* In a large stockpot, heat the olive oil over medium heat and sauté the onions until they are translucent. Add the garlic and red pepper flakes and sauté for about 5 minutes, or until the onions are glazed.

6. Add the chicken stock and bring the soup to a boil over high heat. Add the carrots, celery, onions, and zucchini, lower the heat, and simmer for about 1½ hours, or until the vegetables are tender.

7. Add the meatballs and escarole and simmer for 20 minutes. Stir in the cheese and season to taste with salt. Serve warm.

Marion's mother, Rose, and her maid of honor in 1935.

POLENTA WITH PORTOBELLO MUSHROOMS AND GOAT CHEESE

6 SERVINGS

This polenta can be served with various toppings—such as zucchini, Bolognese sauce, mushrooms, and peas—or with no topping at all. All are equally rich, creamy, and delicious.

FOR THE POLENTA

- 3 cups MILK
- 1 cup WATER
- 1 cup instant POLENTA
- ½ cup MASCARPONE

FOR THE MUSHROOMS

- 6 large PORTOBELLO MUSHROOMS
- 2 tablespoons OLIVE OIL
- SALT and PEPPER
- 6 sprigs fresh ROSEMARY

FOR THE BALSAMIC GLAZE

- 1 cup BALSAMIC VINEGAR
- 4 tablespoons BUTTER
- 6 ¼-inch-thick slices GOAT CHEESE
- 6 sprigs FLAT-LEAF PARSLEY

1. *To make the polenta:* In a large pot over medium heat, bring the milk and water to a boil, then slowly add the polenta. Lower the heat and stir constantly for 6 to 7 minutes, or until the liquid has been absorbed.

2. Remove from the heat and stir in the mascarpone. Set the polenta aside.

3. *To make the mushrooms:* Preheat the oven to 425°F. Break off the stems of the mushrooms and spoon out the gills. Arrange the mushrooms with the olive oil and season with salt and pepper to taste. Arrange the mushrooms on a nonstick sheet pan and place a sprig of rosemary under each one.

4. Bake for 8 to 10 minutes, or until tender. Cool in the pan, slice, and set aside.

5. *To make the balsamic glaze:* In a small saucepan, bring the vinegar to a boil over medium heat and simmer until reduced by half. Remove from the heat, and whisk in the butter.

6. Spoon the polenta into 6 small soup bowls. Garnish each serving with sliced mushrooms and top with a slice of goat cheese. Drizzle with balsamic glaze and garnish with a parsley sprig.

FRESCO
Scotto

In 1993, Rosanna, Anthony Jr., Elaina, and I decided to open a restaurant. We searched for months for the right location. In July of that year we found a perfect space that was owned and operated by Burt Resnick.

After weeks of negotiations between the Resnick lawyers and myself, we finally scheduled the signing of the lease. When I arrived for this meeting with my lawyer, I was surprised to find eight men from the Resnick office seated around a big table.

We negotiated for hours and couldn't come to an agreement. They wanted assurances from me that if I couldn't pay my rent, I would hand over the keys and walk away. Since I didn't have any prior restaurant experience, it was difficult to convince them that we would be a success. I had to defend myself and promise them everything they wanted to hear. Suddenly the door opened and Burt Resnick came in. He looked at everyone and said . . . I *want this lease signed now!*

We signed and that was the start of Fresco by Scotto restaurant.

Whenever Burt and Judy Resnick come for dinner, their favorite is Fritto Misto.

—*Marion*

FRITTO MISTO

6 SERVINGS

This is the grandchildren's favorite dish. They love to coat the vegetables and fish with flour.

- 1 gallon CANOLA OIL
- 1 cup ALL-PURPOSE FLOUR
- 1 cup SEMOLINA
- 1 tablespoon POWDERED ONION
- 2 tablespoons POWDERED GARLIC
- 2 tablespoons PAPRIKA
- SALT and PEPPER
- ½ pound CALAMARI, sliced
- ½ pound BAY SCALLOPS
- ½ pound medium SHRIMP, peeled and deveined
- 1 cup julienned ZUCCHINI (skin on)
- 1 cup julienned YELLOW SQUASH (skin on)
- 2 tablespoons chopped fresh PARSLEY
- 3 LEMONS, each cut in half

1. In a deep fryer, heat the oil to a temperature of 400°F. Keep the oil at this temperature until you are ready to deep-fry the seafood and vegetables.

2. Mix together the flour, semolina, powdered onion, powdered garlic, and paprika. Add salt and pepper to taste.

3. Toss the seafood and julienned vegetables in the flour mixture until they are completely coated. Deep-fry until golden brown. You can fry them in any order, just don't overcrowd the fryer.

4. Place the fritto misto on a serving platter, sprinkle with fresh parsley, and season with salt to taste. Garnish the platter with the lemon halves. Serve warm.

PAPA POMODORO

6 SERVINGS

This is the Italian version of tomato soup—a hearty dish for a cold winter's night.

- 3 tablespoons EXTRA-VIRGIN OLIVE OIL
- 1 tablespoon chopped GARLIC
- 2 cups diced LEEKS
- 1 2-pound can WHOLE TOMATOES, cut and diced, juice reserved
- SALT and PEPPER
- 2 quarts CHICKEN STOCK (see recipe on page 29)
- 3 tablespoons HONEY
- ½ loaf ITALIAN BREAD (9 inches total), cut and diced small
- 1 cup chopped fresh BASIL

1. In a pasta pot, sauté the olive oil and garlic over medium heat for 2 minutes, or until the garlic turns light brown. Add the leeks and sauté for about 5 minutes, or until soft.

2. Add the diced tomatoes and juice. Season with salt and pepper to taste. Add the chicken stock and simmer over low heat for about 30 minutes, or until you see the soup start to thicken.

3. Add the honey, bread, and basil. Season with salt and pepper to taste, and let the soup rest for approximately half an hour before serving. Quickly reheat and serve immediately.

GRILLED PIZZA MARGHERITA

12 PIZZAS

Before we served this pizza at Fresco by Scotto, we used to make it on the barbecue at our country home. The secret is making sure that your grill is oiled and piping hot. Many of our customers love to begin their meal with Grilled Pizza Margherita.

After we wrote our first cookbook, Jeff Zucker (formerly executive producer of NBC's Today *show) came in for lunch and thought it would be a great idea to put one of us on the air for a cooking segment. Little did he know that there's never just one, we come as a family.*

Jeff said it was impossible to have a five-minute cooking segment with four people. I promised that it was possible, and he believed in us. Since then we have been regulars on the Today *show, and Jeff Zucker is our hero!*

We made Pizza Margherita for our first appearance on Today.

—Elaina

- 1 quart lukewarm WATER
- 1 teaspoon fresh YEAST
- 1 tablespoon MOLASSES
- 2½ tablespoons KOSHER SALT
- 1 cup plus 12 tablespoons OLIVE OIL
- 3 cups ALL-PURPOSE FLOUR
- 3 cups HIGH-GLUTEN FLOUR
- ½ cup WHOLE WHEAT FLOUR
- 1 cup grated PECORINO ROMANO CHEESE
- 1 cup grated BEL PAESE CHEESE
- 1 cup TOMATO SAUCE (see recipe on page 29)
- 6 tablespoons chopped fresh PARSLEY
- ½ cup chopped fresh BASIL

1. In a mixing bowl, combine the water, yeast, and molasses. Mix together gently until all the yeast dissolves. Set the mixture aside for 5 to 10 minutes, or until the yeast makes a raft and bubbles. Stir in the salt and 1 cup of the olive oil.

2. With the mixer on a low speed, add the three kinds of flour. Mix until all the flour is absorbed and the dough pulls away from the side of the bowl. Roll the dough into one large ball and let it stand for 5 minutes.

3. Cut the dough into 12 pieces. Roll the pieces into balls and place them on an oiled baking sheet. Brush the balls lightly with olive oil and cover with plastic wrap.

4. If you are going to use the dough right away, let it sit at room temperature for 30 minutes before baking. If you don't need the dough immediately, you can store it for one day in the refrigerator, but you must let it sit at room temperature for 1 hour before using.

5. In a bowl, combine the cheeses.

6. When the dough is ready, prepare the fire, preferably a charcoal fire, but a gas grill works nicely too. Make sure the grill is set at least 4 inches from the fire.

continued

7. On an oiled surface, push a piece of dough out using the palms of your hands. If the dough is sticking to the surface, lift it and drizzle a little more oil on the surface. You want the dough to be a 12-inch circle and paper-thin. The shape of the pizza is not as important as the thickness of the dough.

8. Gently lift the dough and, being careful not to tear it, drape it onto the hot spot of the grill. The dough will start to rise immediately. After about 2 minutes, carefully lift the edge of the dough to see the color of the underside, which should be an even golden brown.

9. Flip the dough over and place it on the side of the grill or a cooler spot of the grill. Brush the cooked side of the dough with olive oil. Take 2½ tablespoons of the cheese and evenly spread it out to the very edge of the dough. Next, with a tablespoon, drop tomato sauce on the pizza (8 to 10 dollops)—you don't want to spread the sauce over the whole surface of the pizza. Drizzle the pizza with 1 tablespoon of extra-virgin olive oil and sprinkle with ½ tablespoon of chopped parsley.

10. Carefully slide the pizza back to the edge of the hot section of the grill, and rotate the pizza until the bottom is evenly golden brown. This should take 3 to 4 minutes. Do not put the pizza directly over the fire, because the bottom will burn before the cheese melts.

11. Garnish with the chopped basil and serve immediately.

MOZZARELLA IN CARROZZA

4 SANDWICHES

This is the Italian version of a grilled cheese sandwich.

- 3 pounds fresh PLUM TOMATOES (about 15), halved
- 1 cup chopped fresh BASIL
- 1 tablespoon chopped GARLIC
- 3½ cups EXTRA-VIRGIN OLIVE OIL
- SALT and PEPPER
- 8 slices crusty ITALIAN BREAD, cut thick
- 1½ pounds fresh MOZZARELLA, sliced ½ inch thick
- 1 cup chopped fresh BASIL LEAVES
- ¼ cup ANCHOVY FILLETS in oil
- 1 cup ALL-PURPOSE FLOUR
- 4 EGGS, lightly beaten
- 2 cups whole MILK
- 3 cups seasoned dried BREAD CRUMBS (store-bought)
- 3 cups TOMATO SAUCE (see recipe on page 79)

1. Preheat the oven to 250°F.

2. In a large bowl, combine the tomatoes, basil, garlic, and ½ cup of the olive oil. Add salt and pepper to taste. Mix well.

3. Arrange the seasoned tomatoes facedown on a nonstick baking sheet. Roast the tomatoes for 2 to 3 hours, or until very soft. Place the tomatoes in a shallow pan and cover to keep the moisture and flavor in.

4. Take a slice of bread and layer on it a slice of mozzarella, tomatoes, basil, anchovies, and salt and pepper to taste. Top with another slice of bread and press together firmly to make a sandwich. Repeat with the rest of the bread and ingredients to make four sandwiches, and set aside.

5. Place the flour in a shallow bowl. In a second shallow bowl, combine the eggs and milk with salt and pepper to taste. In a third shallow bowl, blend the bread crumbs with salt and pepper to taste. Dip the sandwich first in the flour, then in the egg-milk mixture, and then in the bread crumbs.

6. Heat the tomato sauce over low heat until warm.

7. In a sauté pan, heat the remaining 3 cups olive oil over medium to high heat to 250°F. Deep-fry the sandwich until it has a golden brown crust. Spoon the tomato sauce over the top and serve immediately.

POTATO AND ZUCCHINI CHIPS

6 SERVINGS

Seven years ago I visited my cousins Elaine and Vincent Marino in South Carolina. The dish I enjoyed most on that trip was homemade potato chips with blue cheese. When I returned to New York, Potato and Zucchini Chips were born. The chips are now one of our most popular appetizers. Recently, when I visited Charleston, South Carolina, my cousins took me to many new restaurants that not only were beautiful but had exciting and wonderful food. It's nice to know that you don't have to go to Italy to be inspired by talented chefs. —Marion

- 1 pound large BAKING POTATOES
- ½ pound large ZUCCHINI
- 2 tablespoons ALL-PURPOSE FLOUR
- 2 quarts CANOLA OIL for frying
- KOSHER SALT
- 1 cup crumbled GORGONZOLA CHEESE

1. Peel the potatoes and cut them into very thin slices. Immediately put the slices into a bowl of cold water to cover.

2. Cut the zucchini into thin slices, place them in a large bowl, and toss with the flour.

3. In a deep fryer, heat the oil to 325°F.

4. Drain the water from the potatoes and let them dry on paper towels.

5. Deep-fry the potatoes for 2 to 3 minutes, or until golden brown. Drain, season with salt, and let cool.

6. Deep-fry the zucchini for 2 minutes, or until light brown. Drain, season with salt, and let cool.

7. Preheat the oven to 350°F. Place the potato and zucchini chips on a baking sheet and sprinkle with the Gorgonzola. Bake until the cheese has melted, about 5 minutes. Serve immediately.

Anthony Sr. and Marion with Elaine and Vincent Marino in Rome, 1975.

VEAL STOCK

2 QUARTS

- 8 pounds VEAL BONES
- ½ cup EXTRA-VIRGIN OLIVE OIL
- 2 large ONIONS, diced
- 3 large CARROTS, diced
- 1½ 6-ounce cans TOMATO PASTE
- 5 cups DRY RED WINE
- 3 CELERY STALKS, diced
- 3 sprigs FRESH THYME or 1 tablespoon DRIED THYME
- 1 whole GARLIC BULB, cut in half
- 3 BAY LEAVES
- 2 tablespoons whole BLACK PEPPERCORNS

1. Preheat the oven to 350°F. Place the veal bones in a roasting pan and roast for 20 to 30 minutes.

2. In a large sauté pan over medium heat, heat the olive oil. Add the onions and carrots and sauté until golden brown, about 2 minutes. Add the tomato paste and cook for 5 to 9 minutes, or until soft. Add the red wine and celery and cook over low heat for 8 to 12 minutes, or until wine is reduced completely.

3. Place all the ingredients—the cooked vegetables and their liquid, the veal bones, and the thyme, garlic, bay leaves, and peppercorns—into a large stockpot. Add enough water to reach 3 inches above the ingredients.

4. Bring to a boil over high heat, then reduce to a simmer. Skim all the fat from the surface of the liquid. Simmer for 5 to 8 hours to extract the veal flavor from the bones and achieve a thick consistency as a base for your sauces. Skim the surface of the stock every hour or so.

5. When the stock is ready, strain it through a colander into a second stockpot, cool in an ice bath (fill a sink with ice water and put the stockpot in it), and then refrigerate. The stock can be refrigerated for 2 to 3 days or can be kept in the freezer for about 2 weeks.

CHICKEN STOCK

2 QUARTS

- 8 pounds CHICKEN BONES (necks, backs, and wings)
- 2 large ONIONS, diced
- 3 large CARROTS, diced
- 3 CELERY STALKS, diced
- 3 sprigs FRESH THYME or 1 tablespoon DRIED THYME
- 3 BAY LEAVES
- 2 tablespoons whole BLACK PEPPERCORNS
- 1 whole GARLIC BULB, cut in half
- 1 gallon WATER

1. Wash the chicken bones very well.

2. In a large pot over high heat, add all the ingredients and bring to a boil.

3. Reduce the heat and simmer for about 1 hour. Skim all the fat from the surface of the liquid. Set aside to cool.

4. When the stock is cool, strain it through a colander into a second stockpot, cool in an ice bath (fill a sink with ice water and put the stockpot in it), and then refrigerate. The stock can be refrigerated for 2 to 3 days or can be kept in the freezer for about 2 weeks.

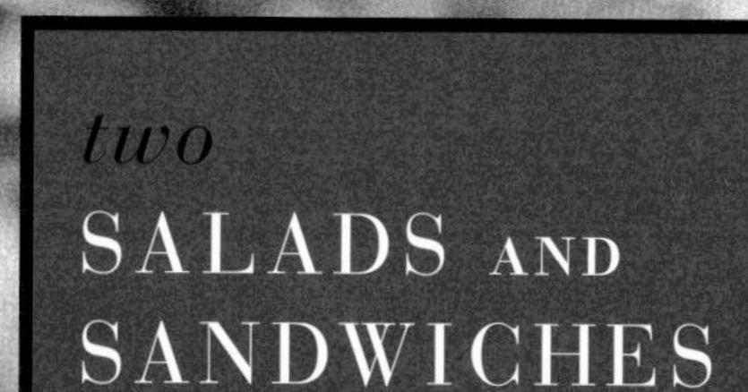

two

SALADS AND SANDWICHES

SOME OF THESE SALAD AND SANDWICH IDEAS ARE QUICK AND SIMPLE, AND OTHERS ARE MORE COMPLICATED AND A BIT MORE FANCY. WE WANTED TO KEEP THE MAJORITY OF THE DISHES LIGHT, TASTY, AND UNIQUE. WE HOPE YOU ENJOY THEM.

* * * * * * * * * * * *

PASTA SALAD CAPRESE STYLE

4 SERVINGS

We ate this great summer dish on the Isle of Capri. It can be served as either a side dish or a main course.

- 1 tablespoon chopped GARLIC
- 4 tablespoons EXTRA-VIRGIN OLIVE OIL
- 2 cups diced PLUM TOMATOES
- Pinch of SALT and PEPPER
- Pinch of RED PEPPER FLAKES
- 1 pound PENNE PASTA, cooked
- 2 cups diced fresh MOZZARELLA
- ½ cup grated PARMESAN CHEESE
- ½ cup chopped fresh BASIL

1. In a large sauté pan over medium heat, sauté the garlic in the olive oil until it browns lightly, about 2 minutes. Add the diced tomatoes and sauté, stirring, for about 2 minutes, or until tomatoes are heated through. Take off the heat. Stir in the salt, pepper, and red pepper.

2. Toss in the pasta, mozzarella, Parmesan, and basil. Finish seasoning with salt and pepper to taste. Serve hot or at room temperature.

TUNA RICE SALAD

6 SERVINGS

This is a great dish to prepare for a busy day.

Jennifer Aniston became a regular when she was in town filming a movie. One day she walked in with a black eye. We all got upset, but only Marion took action. She had the nerve to ask Jennifer if she needed help. Jennifer started laughing and explained that it was just makeup for a scene. I guess she won't be ordering her tuna black and blue. —Elaina

FOR THE LEMON DRESSING

- 1½ cups EXTRA-VIRGIN OLIVE OIL
- ½ cup SHERRY WINE VINEGAR
- Juice from 2 LEMONS
- 4 tablespoons chopped fresh PARSLEY
- SALT and PEPPER

FOR THE TUNA RICE SALAD

- 1 cup WATER
- ½ cup uncooked WHITE RICE
- 1 pound solid WHITE TUNA
- 1 cup diced TOMATOES
- ½ cup pitted KALAMATA OLIVES
- 1 tablespoon CAPERS
- SALT and PEPPER
- ½ pound MESCLUN GREENS

1. *To make the lemon dressing:* In a medium bowl, combine the olive oil, vinegar, lemon juice, and parsley. Blend together slowly with a hand whisk. Season to taste with salt and pepper and set aside.

2. *To make the tuna rice salad:* Bring the water to a boil and add the rice. Allow it to simmer, covered, until the water is absorbed, 12 to 15 minutes. Spread the rice on a cookie sheet to cool.

3. In a bowl, mix the cooled rice, tuna, tomatoes, olives, and capers. Add ¾ of the lemon dressing, toss well, and season to taste with salt and pepper.

4. In a serving bowl, place a layer of mesclun greens, add the tuna-rice mixture, and toss with the remaining lemon dressing.

PASTA SALAD WITH CANNELLINI BEANS AND ARUGULA

6 SERVINGS

This is a great dish for a summer barbecue. You can make it ahead of time and let it sit at room temperature.

- ¾ cup uncooked WHITE CANNELLINI BEANS
- 1 BAY LEAF
- 2 pounds uncooked FUSILLI PASTA
- 2 tablespoons chopped GARLIC
- ¾ cup EXTRA-VIRGIN OLIVE OIL
- ¼ cup TOMATO SAUCE (see recipe on page 79)
- ¼ cup chopped fresh BASIL
- 2 cups blanched, skinned, seedless, diced TOMATOES (about 10 plum tomatoes)
- 2 bunches BABY ARUGULA
- ¼ cup grated PARMIGIANO REGGIANO CHEESE, plus additional, shaved, for garnish
- SALT and PEPPER

1. Bring 4 cups of salted water to a boil. Add the cannellini beans and bay leaf. Simmer until the beans are tender, 20 to 25 minutes.

2. Bring 4 quarts of salted water to a boil. Add the pasta and cook until it is al dente. Drain and cool.

3. In a large sauté pan over low heat, sauté the garlic in the oil until it is lightly brown, about 2 minutes. Add the beans, tomato sauce, fresh basil, and fresh tomatoes and simmer for 5 minutes.

4. Toss in the pasta, 1 bunch of the arugula, and the grated cheese. Season with salt and pepper to taste.

5. Place the salad on a bed of the remaining bunch of arugula and garnish with the shaved Parmigiano Reggiano.

Marion's grandmother with her children.

PANZANELLA SALAD

6 SERVINGS

This is a wonderful dish for a buffet dinner. It tastes great, looks beautiful, and can be prepared hours before you serve it.

FOR THE DRESSING

2 tablespoons fresh LEMON JUICE

3 tablespoons RED WINE VINEGAR

1 cup chopped CAPERS

1 tablespoon DIJON MUSTARD

1 cup EXTRA-VIRGIN OLIVE OIL

SALT and PEPPER

FOR THE PANZANELLA VEGETABLES

2 cups diced RED PEPPERS

2 cups diced YELLOW PEPPERS

1 cup diced RED ONIONS

1 cup diced RED TOMATOES

2 cups diced CUCUMBER

1 cup chopped CELERY

1 cup chopped fresh BASIL

1 loaf ITALIAN or DAY-OLD BREAD (about 18 inches), diced and toasted

SALT and PEPPER

3 bunches BELGIAN ENDIVE

FOR THE GARNISH (OPTIONAL)

ONION RINGS

CAPERS

BASIL OIL

1. *To make the dressing:* Mix the lemon juice, red wine vinegar, capers, and mustard in a blender at a low speed. Slowly pour the oil into the mixture to combine all the ingredients. Add salt and pepper to taste.

2. *To make the panzanella vegetables:* In a large bowl, mix all the ingredients except the Belgian endive. Stir in 1 cup of the dressing. Let the mixture marinate for a half hour at room temperature.

3. Before serving, add salt and pepper to taste. Decorate the salad plates with leaves of the Belgian endive arranged in a star shape, then place panzanella salad in the center of each plate. Garnish with crisp onion rings, capers, and basil oil if you wish.

Marion's mother in costume.

MEATBALL SANDWICH

6 SERVINGS

This is one of the hottest-selling sandwiches at Fresco on the Go. It's great for kids as well as adults. As a matter of fact, when we first opened our restaurant in midtown Manhattan, we decided not to serve pasta with meatballs because we thought it didn't fit the area.

Wouldn't you know it, Regis and Joy Philbin came in, and what was Regis craving? Meatballs! I went into the kitchen and tried to improvise. I didn't have chopped meat, so I used fresh tuna. Regis knew something was fishy, and the next day he teased me relentlessly about the Tuna Balls on Regis & Kathie Lee. *We still don't have spaghetti and meatballs on the menu at the main restaurant, but you can find plenty of meatballs at Fresco on the Go. —Anthony*

- 2 slices BREAD
- ½ cup MILK
- 2 pounds ground BEEF
- 1 cup finely chopped ONIONS
- 3 tablespoons chopped fresh PARSLEY
- 2 EGGS
- 4 tablespoons grated PARMESAN CHEESE
- 1½ tablespoons chopped GARLIC
- SALT and PEPPER
- 3 tablespoons OLIVE OIL
- 6 SESAME BUNS
- 2 cups TOMATO SAUCE, warmed (see recipe on page 79)

1. Soak the bread in the milk. In a medium bowl, mix the ground beef, soaked bread, onions, parsley, eggs, cheese, and garlic. Add salt and pepper to taste. If the mixture is dry, add ½ cup of cold water and mix well. Form into about 12 meatballs.

2. Place the meatballs in a sauté pan with the olive oil and fry over medium to high heat until brown, 10 to 15 minutes.

3. Cut the sesame buns in half. Add tomato sauce and 2 meatballs per sandwich. Serve hot.

HOT PRESSED SOFT-SHELL CRAB CIABATTINI SANDWICH

4 TO 6 SERVINGS

This is a wonderful sandwich to make for your friends, but be prepared to get your hands dirty.

FOR THE CRABS

- 3 EGGS
- 1 tablespoon chopped fresh PARSLEY
- 1 cup ALL-PURPOSE FLOUR
- 1 cup CORNMEAL
- SALT and PEPPER
- 6 soft-shell CRABS, cleaned
- ¼ cup EXTRA-VIRGIN OLIVE OIL
- 1 tablespoon BUTTER

FOR THE LEMON-CAPER AIOLI

- ¼ cup EXTRA-VIRGIN OLIVE OIL
- 4 whole cloves GARLIC
- 3 tablespoons fresh LEMON JUICE
- 1 teaspoon CAPERS
- 1 cup MAYONNAISE
- SALT and PEPPER

FOR THE LEMON WHEELS

- ½ cup ALL-PURPOSE FLOUR
- 1 LEMON, sliced into thin wheels and seeded

FOR THE SANDWICHES

- 6 CIABATTINI ROLLS or any crusty ITALIAN ROLL
- 2 AVOCADOS, sliced
- 3 ROMA TOMATOES, sliced
- 1 pound homemade MOZZARELLA, sliced

1. *To make the crabs:* In a bowl, mix the eggs and parsley and set aside.

2. On a plate, mix ¾ cup of the flour and all the cornmeal. Season the mixture with salt and pepper to taste.

3. Dust the crabs in the remaining ¼ cup flour, dip into the egg, and coat them with the cornmeal mixture.

4. In a medium sauté pan, heat the olive oil and butter over medium heat and sauté the crabs on each side for 4 minutes, or until golden brown. Set the crabs aside.

5. *To make the lemon-caper aioli:* Heat the oil over medium heat and sauté the garlic slowly until golden brown, about 2 minutes. Reserve the oil. Press the garlic with a fork until it is smooth and forms a paste.

6. In a medium bowl, add the lemon juice, capers, mayonnaise, and 1 tablespoon of the reserved olive oil. Add in garlic paste and whisk to a smooth consistency. Season with salt and pepper to taste. Set aside.

7. *To make the lemon wheels:* Lightly flour the lemon slices. Sauté them in 3 tablespoons of the reserved olive oil over medium heat until golden brown, about 1 minute. Let them cool on paper towels. Set aside.

8. *To make the sandwiches:* Slice a ciabattini roll in half and brush both sides with lemon-caper aioli. Layer with a soft-shell crab, avocado, tomato, lemon wheels, and mozzarella. Repeat for the remaining rolls.

9. Place the sandwiches in a hot sauté pan and press them down with a heavy dish until flat. Cook each side for approximately 3 minutes, or until the cheese starts to melt. Serve immediately.

FRIED OYSTER SALAD

6 SERVINGS

This sexy dish gets you in the mood. Every year we serve it on Valentine's Day at Fresco.

FOR THE SALAD

1 pound mixed BABY GREENS

1 tablespoon julienned FENNEL

¾ pound BABY STRING BEANS, blanched

8 CHERRY TOMATOES, cut in half

SALT and PEPPER

¾ cup EXTRA-VIRGIN OLIVE OIL

¼ cup BALSAMIC VINEGAR

FOR THE FRIED OYSTERS

1 cup ALL-PURPOSE FLOUR

3 EGG WHITES

SALT and PEPPER

½ cup BEER

18 fresh OYSTERS, shells reserved

2 cups VEGETABLE OIL or other FRYING OIL

1. *To make the salad:* In a bowl, combine the baby greens, fennel, string beans, tomatoes, salt and pepper to taste, olive oil, and balsamic vinegar, and toss. Set aside.

2. *To make the fried oysters:* In a bowl, combine the flour, egg whites, and salt and pepper to taste. Mix well. Pour the beer in slowly and mix well. Set the batter aside.

3. Open the oysters. Save the shells. Soak the oysters in the batter. Heat the frying oil to 375°F and fry the oysters until crisp on the outside, or about 30 minutes.

4. To serve, set the salad on 6 plates and top each plate with 2 fried oysters and 1 oyster on the half shell.

ARTICHOKE SALAD

6 SERVINGS

If you love artichokes, this is a great way to eat them without a lot of work or a lot of calories.

- 2 heads BELGIAN ENDIVE
- 1 large head RADICCHIO
- 1 bunch ARUGULA
- 6 medium ARTICHOKES
- SALT
- ½ cup OLIVE OIL
- 3 cloves GARLIC
- 1 tablespoon LEMON JUICE
- PEPPER
- ¼ cup BALSAMIC VINEGAR
- 24 slices shaved PARMIGIANO REGGIANO
- 1 cup diced TOMATOES

1. Thoroughly wash and dry the lettuces. Cut all the lettuces into a chiffonade.

2. In a large pot, cover the artichokes just halfway with salted water. Add 2 tablespoons of the olive oil and the garlic. Simmer on medium heat, covered, until the artichokes are tender, about 20 minutes.

3. Clean the artichokes by removing all the leaves. Put aside some of the tender inner leaves for use as a garnish. Remove the "choke" (fuzzy inside) with a spoon and peel the stems.

4. Cut the artichoke bottoms lengthwise into quarters and marinate in 1 tablespoon olive oil, the lemon juice, and a pinch of salt and pepper.

5. Toss the lettuces in the balsamic vinegar and remaining 5 tablespoons olive oil.

6. Mound the lettuces high on 6 plates. Garnish each plate with 4 artichoke quarters and 4 pieces of shaved Parmesan. Arrange artichoke leaves around the plates and sprinkle with diced tomatoes. Season with salt and pepper to taste.

Marion *(second from right)* in Florida in the 1940s with her aunt Josie, cousin Elaine, mom, and cousin Joe.

WINTER SALAD WITH ROASTED PUMPKIN AND OYSTER MUSHROOMS

6 SERVINGS

Thanksgiving has always been a very special holiday for our family. My sons lived in California for many years, Rosanna lived in Manhattan, and Elaina attended college in Washington, D.C., but no matter where they were, they always returned home for Thanksgiving dinner, and I always cooked a feast fit for a king. We spent the day dining, laughing, and reminiscing. Now that we have Fresco, we celebrate at the restaurant with the children and grandchildren. What could be better than that?

This winter salad is a great way to begin your Thanksgiving dinner. —Marion

FOR THE VEGETABLES

- 1 small PUMPKIN (or BUTTERNUT SQUASH if you prefer)
- 5 tablespoons EXTRA-VIRGIN OLIVE OIL
- 4 tablespoons firmly packed BROWN SUGAR
- SALT and PEPPER
- ½ pound OYSTER MUSHROOMS, sliced
- 2 tablespoons ALL-PURPOSE FLOUR
- 1 cup CANOLA OIL for deep frying

FOR THE DRESSING

- ¼ cup SHERRY WINE VINEGAR
- ¾ cup EXTRA-VIRGIN OLIVE OIL
- 1 tablespoon DIJON MUSTARD
- SALT and PEPPER

- 1 pound BABY ARUGULA
- ¼ pound PARMESAN CHEESE, shaved and broken into pieces
- SALT and PEPPER

1. Preheat the oven to 350°F.

2. *To make the vegetables:* Skin the pumpkin, cut it in half, remove the seeds, and dice the flesh into ½-inch squares.

3. In a bowl, mix the pumpkin, 2 tablespoons of the olive oil, brown sugar, and salt and pepper to taste. Spread the mixture on a baking sheet, and roast for 10 to 20 minutes, or until golden brown. Set aside.

4. Divide the oyster mushrooms into two equal portions. In a sauté pan over medium heat, heat the remaining 3 tablespoons of olive oil and sauté half of the mushrooms until golden brown.

5. Lightly flour the remaining mushrooms and set aside. In a deep fryer, heat the canola oil to 350°F and cook the floured mushrooms until crispy, 3 to 5 minutes. Place the mushrooms on a paper towel to drain. Season with salt.

6. *To make the dressing:* In a bowl, combine the sherry wine vinegar, olive oil, mustard, and salt and pepper to taste. Stir until smooth.

7. In a bowl, mix the arugula, sautéed mushrooms, and roasted pumpkin.

8. Add the sherry vinaigrette and Parmesan cheese. Add salt and pepper to taste. Place the salad on a platter and sprinkle the crispy mushrooms on top.

STRING BEAN AND POTATO SALAD WITH BASIL PESTO

6 SERVINGS

You can serve this salad as an appetizer or as a side dish. It's great hot or cold.

Every year for the last fifteen years my friends and I have gotten together at Mickey and Caryl Palin's home in Southampton for a weekend. Lynn and Jack Schwartz, Jerry and Michelle Wolkoff, and my husband, Anthony, and I look forward to it every summer. We eat, we sing, we dance . . . and we cook!

We promised one another that no matter what happens in our lives, we would always have our annual weekend. We love trying different recipes, but String Bean and Potato Salad with Basil Pesto is a classic in the summer. —Marion

FOR THE BASIL PESTO

- ½ cup PINE NUTS
- ¾ cup plus 1 tablespoon EXTRA-VIRGIN OLIVE OIL
- 3 cloves GARLIC, coarsely chopped
- 2 cups loosely packed fresh BASIL LEAVES
- ½ cup freshly grated PARMESAN CHEESE
- KOSHER SALT to taste

FOR THE STRING BEAN AND POTATO SALAD

- 3 pounds STRING BEANS, cut in half
- 2 pounds YUKON GOLD POTATOES, peeled and cut into cubes
- 1 cup EXTRA-VIRGIN OLIVE OIL
- SALT and PEPPER

1. *To make the basil pesto:* Preheat the oven to 350°F. Spread the pine nuts in a single layer on a baking sheet and toast for 4 to 5 minutes, or until fragrant and golden brown. Shake the pan once or twice during toasting, and take care that the nuts do not burn. Transfer the nuts to a plate to cool.

2. In a blender or food processor fitted with a metal blade, combine ¾ cup of the olive oil, the garlic, 1 cup of the basil, and the pine nuts. Process until nearly smooth. Add the remaining basil and process until nearly smooth. Add the cheese and pulse to combine. Season to taste with salt, pulsing 2 to 3 times just to mix. Use immediately or transfer to a glass or plastic container for storage. Top with the remaining 1 tablespoon of olive oil, cover, and refrigerate.

3. *To make the string bean and potato salad:* In a large pot of salted boiling water, blanch the string beans for 2 to 3 minutes until crunchy. Drain.

4. In another pot of salted boiling water, cook the potatoes until tender, drain, and let them cool down.

5. In a bowl, combine the string beans, potatoes, and 2½ cups of the basil pesto and toss while adding the olive oil and salt and pepper to taste.

6. Place the salad on a platter and serve immediately.

Here are some of our favorite, most versatile dressings for your salads.

BALSAMIC DRESSING

6 SERVINGS

- ½ tablespoon chopped fresh BASIL
- ½ tablespoon chopped fresh OREGANO
- ½ tablespoon chopped fresh THYME
- ½ tablespoon chopped fresh ROSEMARY
- 1 tablespoon minced GARLIC
- 1 tablespoon minced SHALLOTS
- 1 tablespoon DIJON MUSTARD
- 1 tablespoon RED WINE VINEGAR
- ¼ cup BALSAMIC VINEGAR
- ¾ cup OLIVE OIL

Slowly whisk together all the ingredients.

OREGANO VINAIGRETTE DRESSING

6 SERVINGS

- 1 tablespoon chopped fresh OREGANO
- 1 tablespoon minced SHALLOTS
- ½ tablespoon DIJON MUSTARD
- 1 tablespoon SHERRY VINEGAR
- ¼ cup RED WINE VINEGAR
- ¾ cup OLIVE OIL

Slowly whisk together all the ingredients.

LEMON VINAIGRETTE

6 SERVINGS

- 1 tablespoon chopped fresh THYME
- 1 tablespoon chopped fresh PARSLEY
- 1 tablespoon minced GARLIC
- 1 tablespoon minced SHALLOTS
- ½ tablespoon DIJON MUSTARD
- ¼ cup fresh LEMON JUICE
- 1 tablespoon SHERRY VINEGAR
- ¾ cups OLIVE OIL

Slowly whisk together all the ingredients.

CAESAR DRESSING

6 SERVINGS

- 2 ANCHOVY FILLETS
- 1 tablespoon fresh LEMON JUICE
- 1 tablespoon RED WINE VINEGAR
- 1 tablespoon WORCESTERSHIRE SAUCE
- 1 GARLIC CLOVE, minced
- 1 tablespoon DIJON MUSTARD
- ½ cup grated PARMESAN CHEESE
- Dash TABASCO
- 1 cup HELLMANN'S MAYONNAISE

Blend all the ingredients with a hand mixer or blender.

three

PASTAS

THERE IS NOTHING BETTER THAN A GREAT DISH OF PASTA! WE LOVE OUR PASTA AND EAT IT OFTEN. NO MATTER WHAT THE OCCASION, THERE'S ALWAYS A PASTA COURSE. COLD OR HOT, IT'S DELICIOUS AND SO SATISFYING.

TAGLIOLINI WITH ROCK SHRIMP, ZUCCHINI, AND TOASTED BREAD CRUMBS

6 SERVINGS

This easy dish features many different flavors. You'll impress your guests and your family.

FOR THE ZUCCHINI PUREE

1 tablespoon chopped GARLIC

½ ONION, diced

2 ZUCCHINI, diced

1 tablespoon EXTRA-VIRGIN OLIVE OIL

½ cup WHITE WINE

2 cups CLAM JUICE

SALT and PEPPER

FOR THE PASTA

1 pound uncooked TAGLIOLINI PASTA (or spaghetti)

½ tablespoon chopped SHALLOT

1 tablespoon chopped GARLIC

2 ZUCCHINI, diced

6 tablespoons EXTRA-VIRGIN OLIVE OIL

½ pound ROCK SHRIMP, diced

1 cup WHITE WINE

½ cup BUTTER

4 tablespoons TOASTED BREAD CRUMBS (homemade or store-bought)

½ teaspoon RED PEPPER FLAKES

½ cup chopped fresh BASIL

1. *To make the zucchini puree:* In a sauté pan over medium heat, sauté the garlic, onion, and zucchini in the olive oil for 3 to 5 minutes, until golden brown. Add the white wine and simmer until reduced by half. Add the clam juice and simmer until reduced by half again. Add salt and pepper to taste. Puree in a blender and strain through a sieve. Set aside the zucchini puree.

2. *To make the pasta:* Bring a large pot of lightly salted water to a boil. Cook the pasta for 6 minutes, or until al dente. Drain.

3. In a sauté pan over medium heat, cook the shallot, garlic, and zucchini in the olive oil until the zucchini is soft. Add the shrimp and sauté for 3 to 4 minutes, or until the shrimp is pink.

4. Deglaze the pan with the white wine. Add 2 cups of the zucchini puree, the pasta, and the butter and mix very well. If it seems dry, add the remaining puree.

5. Top with the toasted bread crumbs, red pepper flakes, and fresh basil and serve.

FRESCO TIMPANO

6 SERVINGS

This is an Italian version of pot pie, with lots of pasta.

- 1 pound uncooked PENNE PASTA
- 1½ pounds SWEET ITALIAN SAUSAGE, removed from casing
- 2 tablespoons chopped GARLIC
- 4 tablespoons OLIVE OIL
- 1 cup SWEET PEAS
- 2 cups diced TOMATOES
- 1 bunch fresh BASIL
- 2 EGGPLANTS, unskinned, diced
- 2½ cups TOMATO SAUCE (see recipe on page 79)
- 1¼ pounds fresh RICOTTA CHEESE
- 1 cup grated PARMESAN CHEESE
- ½ pound fresh MOZZARELLA, diced
- SALT and PEPPER
- 2 tablespoons ALL-PURPOSE FLOUR
- 2 puff PASTRY SHEETS
- 4 tablespoons BUTTER
- 2 EGG YOLKS, lightly beaten

1. Cook pasta in boiling water until al dente, about 8 minutes. Drain and set aside.

2. In a sauté pan over high heat, cook the sausage, garlic, and 2 tablespoons of the oil until the meat is crispy. Drain the oil.

3. In another pan over medium heat, heat the remaining 2 tablespoons olive oil and sauté the eggplant until crispy, or approximately 5 minutes.

4. In a large bowl, mix together the peas, tomatoes, basil, sausage, and crispy eggplant.

5. Add 2 cups of the tomato sauce and fold in the ricotta, Parmesan, mozzarella, and penne. Add salt and pepper to taste.

6. Preheat the oven to 325°F. Sprinkle the flour on the puff pastry sheets and roll out into 9-inch-diameter circles.

7. Rub the butter on the bottom and sides of a 12-inch springform pan. Line the pan with one pastry sheet and fill it with the penne mixture.

8. Cover with a pastry sheet, making sure that none of the stuffing is left uncovered. Brush the top of the pastry with egg yolks and bake for about 30 minutes, or until golden brown. Warm the remaining ½ cup of tomato sauce. Cut the timpano into wedges and top with the warmed sauce. Serve hot.

SPAGHETTI PIE

6 SERVINGS

A wonderful way to use your leftover pasta.

- 1 pound uncooked SPAGHETTI
- 1 tablespoon chopped GARLIC
- 7 tablespoons OLIVE OIL
- ½ pound SMOKED MOZZARELLA, diced
- ½ pound TOMATOES, skinned, seeded, and diced
- ½ cup chopped BLACK OLIVES
- 4 EGGS, lightly beaten
- ¼ cup julienned fresh BASIL
- 4 tablespoons BUTTER
- 2½ cups grated PARMESAN CHEESE
- 2 whole EGGPLANTS, sliced thin
- 2 tablespoons BALSAMIC VINEGAR
- 1 cup TOMATO SAUCE (see recipe on page 79), warmed
- SALT and PEPPER

1. Bring a large pot of lightly salted water to a boil. Cook the pasta for 6 minutes, or until al dente. Drain and keep warm.

2. In a sauté pan over medium heat, sauté the garlic in 3 tablespoons of the olive oil until golden brown, about 2 minutes.

3. In a large mixing bowl, combine the pasta, sautéed garlic and the oil in which it has cooked, mozzarella, tomatoes, olives, eggs, basil, butter, and 1 cup of the Parmesan cheese.

4. In a large sauté pan over medium heat, sauté the eggplants in the remaining 4 tablespoons olive oil for about 5 minutes, or until soft. Set aside and sprinkle with the balsamic vinegar.

5. Preheat the oven to 350°F. Line the bottom and sides of a 9-inch pie plate with about ¾ of the sautéed eggplants.

6. Pour the pasta filling into the dish, season with salt and pepper, and cover with the remaining sautéed eggplants. Sprinkle 1 cup of Parmesan cheese over the top.

7. Bake for 40 minutes, or until golden brown. Let rest for about 20 minutes.

8. Preheat the broiler. Remove from the mold, flip the pie over onto an ovenproof plate, top with the tomato sauce and the remaining ½ cup of Parmesan cheese, and lightly broil to a golden brown, about 3 minutes.

We get important people from all over the world at our restaurant. One afternoon a woman came in to make a reservation. She told me that her husband was very important and had to sit in the middle of the restaurant. Her name was Maya.

At 5:30 that evening I received a phone call from Maya; she had to cancel the reservation. A few minutes later the door opened and in came four big Israelis with guns protruding from their coats. In the middle of them stood a man. They immediately went to the center of the room and sat.

I was startled. They passed me by like I was a fixture on the wall.

Suddenly, I noticed four Secret Service men talking into their sleeves. I said to one of them, "Who is this man?" He told me that the man was the defense minister of Israel. I said, "Did he have a reservation?" He said that the reservation was under the name of Maya. I didn't know how to tell him that Mrs. Maya had canceled. "I hope you're not fooling with us," he said. I told him that I wouldn't fool around with men carrying so many guns.

The defense minister was informed and he quickly left Fresco. I waved and told him to come back without her the next time. He smiled and agreed.

I am sure that if he had stayed for dinner, he would have ordered Spaghetti Pie!

—*Marion*

BLACK WINTER TRUFFLE AND RED BEET RAVIOLI

6 SERVINGS

This ravioli is perfect for Valentine's Day because of its unusual filling. The flavors really complement one another.

FOR THE PASTA SHEETS

- 3 cups ALL-PURPOSE FLOUR
- 2 EGGS, beaten thoroughly
- 1 teaspoon EXTRA-VIRGIN OLIVE OIL
- ¼ teaspoon SALT

FOR THE FILLING

- 1 pound RED BEETS, peeled and cut into ¼-inch dice
- ¼ cup plus a drizzle EXTRA-VIRGIN OLIVE OIL
- ½ pound fresh SPINACH
- 1 tablespoon chopped GARLIC
- 2 tablespoons chopped SHALLOTS
- ½ pound fresh RICOTTA CHEESE
- ½ cup GOAT CHEESE
- 4 tablespoons BLACK TRUFFLES, pureed
- SALT and PEPPER
- ½ cup UNSALTED BUTTER, melted
- ¼ cup grated PARMESAN CHEESE

1. *To make the pasta sheets:* Place the flour in the center of a work surface and make a well. Mix the eggs, oil, and salt. Pour into the center of the flour well.

2. Fold the flour into the eggs and knead into a ball. Add 1 tablespoon of cold water if the dough seems too dry. Cover with plastic wrap and refrigerate the dough for at least 4 hours before rolling out.

3. *To make the filling:* Preheat the oven to 350°F. Lay the beets on a sheet of aluminum foil, top with a drizzle of extra-virgin olive oil, and seal the beets in the foil package. Roast for about 45 minutes, or until soft. Cool the beets in the foil package and mince to a smooth texture.

4. In a sauté pan over medium heat, sauté the spinach with the garlic, shallots, and the remaining 1/4 cup olive oil for 2 minutes, or until wilted. Chop the spinach mixture and squeeze to remove all the liquid.

5. In a bowl, place the beets, spinach, ricotta, goat cheese, and black truffles. Mix well; the texture should be firm. Add salt and pepper to taste.

6. Using a pasta machine, roll out the pasta on the thinnest setting and cut it into 6 sheets, each about 16 inches long each. Do not roll out too many sheets at a time or the dough will begin to dry and will be difficult to handle. Keep the sheets under a damp cloth so that they don't dry out.

7. Lay one pasta sheet on a clean work surface. Make a row of 5 generous teaspoons of filling, 1 inch apart, across the center of 1 pasta sheet. Carefully fold the sheet in half toward you, matching the horizontal edges of the dough. With your fingertips, gently press down around the teaspoons of filling and along the 3 sides of the folded pasta sheet to seal the ravioli.

8. Using a pasta cutter, trim off the edges of the dough and cut apart the ravioli. Gently crimp the edges of the ravioli with a fork. Lay the ravioli on a lightly floured bedsheet or tea towels. Let dry at least 5 minutes before cooking. Repeat with the rest of the pasta sheets and filling.

9. Bring a large pot of salted water to a boil. Add ravioli to the boiling water. Very fresh pasta takes 2 to 5 minutes to cook. The ravioli are done when they come to the surface.

10. Carefully drain the ravioli and transfer to a warm serving platter. Top with the unsalted butter and serve with the Parmesan cheese.

RISOTTO WITH WILD MUSHROOMS

6 SERVINGS

When mushrooms are added to a creamy risotto, their earthy flavor is enhanced.

For many years during the summer, my cousins Elaine Marino and Joe Lacqua and I got together and cooked. I was never blessed with a sister or brother, but my cousins are as close to me as any sibling could have been. This recipe is one of Joe's favorites. He considers himself a chef. I love him dearly, but a chef he is not!

—Marion

- ½ cup dried PORCINI MUSHROOMS
- 3 tablespoons BUTTER
- 1 pound WILD MUSHROOMS, sliced (MORELS, SHIITAKE, or other)
- SALT and PEPPER
- 2½ quarts CHICKEN STOCK (see recipe on page 29)
- ½ cup OLIVE OIL
- 6 GARLIC CLOVES, chopped
- ½ ONION, diced
- 2 cups uncooked ARBORIO or CARNAROLLI RICE
- ½ cup DRY WHITE WINE
- ¾ cup grated PARMIGIANO REGGIANO CHEESE
- 3 tablespoons chopped fresh PARSLEY

1. Soak the dried porcini mushrooms in 1½ cups of very hot water for 20 minutes, or until plumped. Drain the mushrooms and chop fine. Set aside.

2. In a sauté pan over medium heat, melt the butter and cook the wild mushrooms for 3 minutes, or until soft. Season with salt and pepper. Set aside.

3. In a stockpot over high heat, bring the chicken stock to a low simmer.

4. In a heavy-bottomed pot, heat the olive oil and sauté the garlic and onion over medium heat until golden brown. Add the rice and stir thoroughly.

5. Add the wine and porcini mushrooms to the pan, stirring constantly.

6. Add 2 cups of the chicken stock and simmer for 15 minutes, stirring constantly to make sure the risotto doesn't stick to the bottom of the pan. When the risotto has absorbed the stock, continue to slowly add more, 2 cups at a time. The goal is to cook the rice and obtain a creamy texture. Add the sautéed mushrooms approximately 3 minutes before the end of the cooking time. Reserve any remaining stock for use in another recipe.

7. Stir in the Parmesan cheese, garnish with the parsley, and serve immediately.

Marion with Joe Lacqua in the 1940s.

CBS-2 reporter Penny Crone was so excited that she was able to arrange a lunch date with police commissioner Ray Kelly at Fresco. She invited Fox News anchor John Roland and me to join her for the interview, but we both had previous engagements. For days Penny anxiously anticipated this lunch. On the appointed day, the commissioner arrived at Fresco—but there was no Penny! Mom frantically called me at home, saying, "Where's Penny?" I called her, and she was watching TV in her bunny pj's. She told me, "Tell your mom to keep him busy till I get there, because I thought the lunch date was tomorrow."

Mom made conversation with the commissioner until Penny arrived, looking glamorous—as if all was normal.

—*Rosanna*

PENNE FROM HEAVEN

6 SERVINGS

This is our version of macaroni and cheese. Many of our customers, including CBS-2 reporter Penny Crone, have told us that when eating this dish, they feel as if they've died and gone to heaven.

- 1 pound uncooked PENNE PASTA
- 1 cup diced PROSCIUTTO
- 3 tablespoons OLIVE OIL
- ½ cup UNSALTED BUTTER
- 1 cup HEAVY CREAM
- 4½ cups grated PARMESAN CHEESE
- PEPPER

1. Bring a large pot of lightly salted water to a boil. Cook the pasta until al dente, or 8 to 10 minutes. Drain and keep warm.

2. In a sauté pan over low heat, sauté the prosciutto in the olive oil for about 3 minutes, or until prosciutto is wilted.

3. Preheat the broiler.

4. In a sauté pan over medium heat, melt the butter. Add the prosciutto, heavy cream, 3½ cups of the Parmesan cheese, and a pinch of pepper.

5. Bring the sauce to a light boil, add the pasta, toss, and transfer the pasta into a shallow baking dish.

6. Sprinkle the remaining 1 cup of Parmesan cheese on top and broil for 5 to 6 minutes, or until golden brown. Serve immediately.

Rosanna with Lynn Schwartz and Penny Crone.

GARGANELLE WITH CHICKEN, EGGPLANT, ARUGULA, AND TOMATO

6 SERVINGS

This is a simple, healthful recipe that has lots of protein and carbohydrates in one dish. We serve it as a special pasta at Fresco.

- 1 pound uncooked GARGANELLE PASTA (or PENNE)
- 1 cup EXTRA-VIRGIN OLIVE OIL
- ½ pound EGGPLANT, diced
- 1 tablespoon chopped GARLIC
- 1 pound CHICKEN BREAST, diced
- ½ pound TOMATOES, diced
- ¼ cup julienned fresh BASIL
- ¼ cup grated PARMESAN CHEESE
- ¼ pound ARUGULA, chopped
- SALT and PEPPER

1. Bring a large pot of lightly salted water to a boil. Cook the pasta for 5 minutes, or until al dente.

2. Drain the pasta and set aside.

3. In a deep sauté pan, heat the oil until hot. Add the eggplant and fry until crispy golden brown, about 5 minutes. Remove the eggplant with a slotted spoon and drain on a paper towel.

4. In the same oil, sauté the garlic for about 2 minutes, add the chicken, and cook for about 4 minutes, or until the chicken is cooked through. Add the tomatoes and basil and cook for 3 more minutes, or until the tomatoes are hot.

5. Add the Parmesan cheese, arugula, and eggplant to the sauce. Season with salt and pepper to taste, and mix with the cooked garganelle pasta.

RISOTTO WITH LOBSTER, SHRIMP, AND CALAMARI

10 SERVINGS

The perfect risotto needs tender loving care, which means stirring constantly and making sure it stays moist.

3 LOBSTERS, 2 pounds each

FOR THE LOBSTER STOCK

3 GARLIC CLOVES

1 cup EXTRA-VIRGIN OLIVE OIL

1 ONION, chopped

1 CARROT, chopped

1 CELERY STALK, chopped

¼ bunch fresh THYME, chopped

¾ cup TOMATO PASTE

1 cup DRY WHITE WINE

8 cups WATER

FOR THE RISOTTO

1 cup EXTRA-VIRGIN OLIVE OIL

2 tablespoons chopped SHALLOTS

1 tablespoon chopped GARLIC

2 cups uncooked ARBORIO or CARNAROLLI RICE

1 cup DRY WHITE WINE

2 cups TOMATO SAUCE (see recipe on page 79)

½ pound SHRIMP, cooked and cut small

½ pound CALAMARI, cooked and cut small

2 tablespoons chopped fresh PARSLEY

1 tablespoon chopped fresh BASIL

SALT and PEPPER

1. In a pot filled with enough boiling water to cover the lobsters, cook lobsters for about 5 minutes. Cool down in ice water, then clean the lobsters: take off the back with a knife, cut the tail in half, crack the claws and legs, and take the meat out. Set the meat aside for the risotto and the shells for the stock.

2. *To make the lobster stock:* In a large stockpot over medium heat, sauté the garlic and lobster shells in the olive oil for 2 minutes. Add the vegetables, thyme, and tomato paste and cook for 10 minutes.

3. Add the wine, reduce by half, and add 8 cups water.

4. Bring to a boil over high heat, lower to medium heat, and simmer for 30 minutes. Strain and cool the liquid; you will have about 4 cups of stock. Set the stock aside.

5. *To make the risotto:* In a pot over medium heat, heat the olive oil and sauté the shallots and garlic until golden brown.

6. Add the rice and stir, making sure to mix the risotto well with the oil.

7. Slowly add 2 cups of the lobster stock and the wine and simmer for 15 minutes, stirring constantly, making sure that the risotto doesn't stick to the bottom of the pan. Continue to add the stock (2 cups at a time) as soon as it's been absorbed, to keep the risotto moist. When the risotto has a creamy texture and it is cooked through, that's when you know you're finished.

8. Add the tomato sauce, lobster, shrimp, calamari, parsley, and basil and continue to stir for approximately 5 more minutes.

9. Add salt and pepper to taste. Serve immediately.

RISOTTO WITH ROASTED WINTER VEGETABLES

6 SERVINGS

You don't have to use these vegetables; you can use your favorites. Depending upon the season, some of our other favorites include cauliflower, broccoli rabe, artichokes, and asparagus.

In 1994, when Rosanna was pregnant with her second child, Louis John (aka L.J.), all she craved was Risotto with Roasted Winter Vegetables. At the time she was a reporter for Fox 5, but the rumor around town was that she was going to be the anchor of the Fox 5 News at 10. *I was happy for Rosanna, but I was also trying to stop her from eating risotto every day. I begged, I cried, but she continued eating! In her eighth month, the rumor became a reality. Rosanna was made anchor, and she was sixty pounds heavier. At one point, we were going to name the baby "Risotto," but Louis John was more appropriate. —Marion*

FOR THE ROASTED MIXED VEGETABLES

- ¼ cup diced ZUCCHINI
- ¼ cup diced BROCCOLI
- ¼ cup diced CARROTS
- ¼ cup diced EGGPLANT
- ½ cup OLIVE OIL
- 1 teaspoon chopped GARLIC

FOR THE RISOTTO

- 1 ONION, finely chopped
- ½ cup EXTRA-VIRGIN OLIVE OIL
- 2 cups uncooked ARBORIO or CARNAROLLI RICE
- ¾ cup DRY WHITE WINE
- 2½ quarts CHICKEN STOCK (see recipe on page 29)
- ½ cup grated PARMESAN CHEESE
- SALT and PEPPER
- ½ cup chopped fresh PARSLEY

1. *To make the roasted vegetables:* Preheat the oven to 350°F. Toss the vegetables with the olive oil and garlic. Place the vegetables in a roasting pan and roast for 10 to 15 minutes, or until soft.

2. *To make the risotto:* Sauté the onion in the olive oil. Add the rice and stir until coated with the oil.

3. Add the wine and ½ cup of the chicken stock, stirring constantly until the liquid is absorbed. Add another ½ cup of the stock and stir for approximately 20 minutes, adding more stock as the risotto absorbs it, until the rice has a creamy texture and is cooked through.

4. Stir in the roasted vegetables and Parmesan cheese. Season with salt and pepper, garnish with the parsley, and serve immediately.

We were asked to do a cooking show on Fox 5's *Good Day New York* with Jim Ryan. We thought this segment would be easy because I work for Fox 5. Instead, it was a comedy of errors.

We had to prepare our food on the set in the dark. My mom tripped on a wire and slid halfway across the studio floor like a baseball player sliding into home plate. When she looked up, Jim Ryan was directly in front of her doing the news. She was startled but decided to get up as quietly as possible and go to the greenroom to compose herself. When she opened the door to the greenroom, she was shocked to find twelve barking dogs that Fox was using for another segment.

Mom then decided to go back into the dark studio only to find all of us on the set hysterical because we forgot to bring the pasta from the restaurant. Anthony quickly went to the corner deli and bought a package of pasta.

When we finally went on the air, we were notified that the show was out of time.

This wasn't our day!

—Rosanna

LINGUINE WITH CLAM SAUCE

4 SERVINGS

Try to find Manila clams for this dish; they're highly prized for their sweet, tender meat.

- 1 pound dried LINGUINE
- 1 cup EXTRA-VIRGIN OLIVE OIL
- 2 teaspoons chopped GARLIC
- 1 cup CLAM JUICE
- 2 tablespoons BUTTER
- 2 tablespoons RED PEPPER FLAKES
- 4 tablespoons chopped PARSLEY
- 2 pounds MANILA or LITTLE NECK CLAMS
- SALT and PEPPER

1. Bring a large pot of lightly salted water to a boil over high heat. Cook the pasta for 8 minutes, or until al dente.

2. Meanwhile, in a large sauté pan over low heat, sauté the olive oil and garlic until golden brown, about 5 minutes.

3. Add the clam juice, butter, red pepper flakes, parsley, and clams. Season with salt and pepper. Cover and cook until the clams open. Discard any unopened clams.

4. Drain the pasta, add it to the pan with the clams, and toss to blend. Serve immediately.

PENNE WITH ARUGULA PESTO

4 SERVINGS

This is Fresco's recipe for pesto. Traditionally it's made with basil; we like to use arugula instead, to give it a peppery flavor.

FOR THE PESTO

- ½ pound PINE NUTS
- ½ pound fresh ARUGULA
- 2 tablespoons chopped GARLIC
- 1 cup EXTRA-VIRGIN OLIVE OIL
- 2 tablespoons LEMON JUICE
- SALT and PEPPER

FOR THE PASTA

- 1 pound uncooked PENNE PASTA
- 1 tablespoon chopped GARLIC
- 1 tablespoon EXTRA-VIRGIN OLIVE OIL
- 2 cups CHICKEN STOCK (see recipe on page 29)
- ¼ cup BUTTER
- SALT and PEPPER
- 1 cup grated PARMESAN CHEESE

1. *To make the pesto:* Preheat the oven to 350°F. Place the pine nuts on a baking sheet and toast in the oven for 3 to 5 minutes.

2. Place the arugula, garlic, and toasted pine nuts into a blender or food processor. Drizzle in the olive oil little by little and puree until smooth. Add the lemon juice and salt and pepper to taste, and puree briefly to blend.

3. *To make the pasta:* Bring a large pot of lightly salted water to a boil. Cook the penne for 8 minutes, or until al dente. Drain.

4. In a sauté pan over low heat, sauté the garlic in the oil until golden brown.

5. Add the chicken stock, butter, and pasta. Season with salt and pepper.

6. Transfer to a serving platter. Toss with the arugula pesto and Parmesan cheese. Serve immediately.

SPAGHETTI WITH LOBSTER AND SHRIMP RAGU

6 SERVINGS

In Venice, we tasted a wonderful seafood pasta with langoustines, but when we re-created it at Fresco we decided to use a combination of lobster and shrimp, because we liked the flavors and texture together.

- 1 tablespoon chopped GARLIC
- ½ cup OLIVE OIL
- 3 cups LOBSTER STOCK (see recipe on page 65)
- 1 quart TOMATO SAUCE (see recipe on page 79)
- ½ tablespoon crushed RED PEPPER
- 1 cup diced LOBSTER MEAT
- 1 cup diced SHRIMP
- ¼ cup chopped fresh BASIL
- 2 tablespoons chopped fresh PARSLEY
- 1½ pounds uncooked SPAGHETTI
- ½ cup BUTTER

1. In a medium sauté pan over medium heat, sauté the garlic in the olive oil until golden brown.

2. Add the lobster stock, tomato sauce, and crushed red pepper. Bring to a boil, lower the heat, and simmer for about 45 minutes, or until the liquid is reduced by half.

3. Add the lobster, shrimp, and basil and simmer for 10 minutes.

4. Bring a large pot of salted water to a boil. Boil the pasta until very al dente and strain.

5. Add the lobster and shrimp sauce to the pasta and stir. Add the butter and stir to melt. Sprinkle with the chopped parsley and serve hot.

THANKSGIVING LASAGNA WITH BRAISED BEEF AND ROASTED PUMPKIN

6 SERVINGS

Italians don't eat just turkey on Thanksgiving; they love to eat pasta, too! You can make this dish a day ahead so that you can focus your attention on roasting your turkey.

- 2 CARROTS, diced
- ½ ONION, chopped
- ½ CELERY STALK, diced
- 2 tablespoons BUTTER

FOR THE BRAISED BEEF

- 2 tablespoons OLIVE OIL
- 1 tablespoon chopped GARLIC
- 2½ pounds ground BEEF
- 1½ cups DRY RED WINE
- ½ can TOMATO PUREE
- 1 cup BEEF BROTH
- SALT and PEPPER
- 1 tablespoon dried ROSEMARY

FOR THE PUMPKIN

- 2 cups fresh PUMPKIN, diced small
- SALT and PEPPER

FOR THE LASAGNA

- 4 fresh PASTA SHEETS (store-bought), or 2 pounds LASAGNA NOODLES
- 2 tablespoons OLIVE OIL
- 2 cups BÉCHAMEL (see recipe on page 80)
- 1½ pounds fresh MOZZARELLA, shredded
- 5 pounds fresh RICOTTA CHEESE
- 2 cups grated PARMESAN CHEESE
- 1 cup grated PECORINO ROMANO CHEESE

1. Sauté the carrots, onion, and celery over medium heat with the butter for about 5 minutes, or until soft. Mince in a food processor and set aside.

2. *To make the braised beef:* In a sauté pan over medium heat, heat the olive oil and sauté the garlic until it is golden brown, about 2 minutes. Add the minced vegetables and cook for 10 minutes more.

3. Add the beef and brown thoroughly. Drain off the fat. Add the wine and reduce by half. Add the tomato puree, broth, salt and pepper to taste, and rosemary and cook for 30 to 45 minutes.

4. *To make the pumpkin:* Preheat the oven to 350°F. Place the pumpkin cubes on a sheet pan and roast for 15 to 20 minutes, or until lightly caramelized. Season with salt and pepper to taste, and set aside to cool.

5. *To make the lasagna:* Bring a large pot of salted water to a boil and add a little olive oil to prevent sticking. Cook the pasta sheets until al dente, drain, and shock in ice-cold water.

6. Preheat the oven to 350°F. Lightly butter an 8- by 12-inch baking pan and layer with a sheet of pasta, ¼ of the béchamel, ⅓ each of the braised beef and roasted pumpkin, ⅓ each of the mozzarella, ricotta, and Parmesan, and ¼ of the Pecorino Romano. Repeat the layering twice, pressing down as you work.

7. Press down once again and layer with pasta, béchamel, and Pecorino Romano cheese. Cover with aluminum foil.

8. Bake for 35 minutes, let stand for 10 minutes, and serve.

Rosie O'Donnell helped us prepare this lasagna for her Thanksgiving show. We had lots of fun working with Rosie. She enjoyed getting involved with the recipes.

—*Elaina*

MEATBALL LASAGNA

6 SERVINGS

My grandchildren love to make their own meatballs. The only problem with this recipe is that the babies eat the meatballs right after they're fried . . . and they never make it into the sauce.
—*Marion*

FOR THE MEATBALLS

- 2 slices BREAD
- ½ cup MILK
- 2 pounds ground BEEF
- 1 cup finely chopped ONIONS
- 3 tablespoons chopped fresh PARSLEY
- 2 EGGS
- 4 tablespoons grated PARMESAN CHEESE
- 1½ tablespoons chopped GARLIC
- SALT and PEPPER
- 3 tablespoons OLIVE OIL
- 5 cups TOMATO SAUCE, warmed (see recipe on page 79)

FOR THE LASAGNA

- 2 pounds fresh MOZZARELLA, diced
- 2 cups grated PARMIGIANO REGGIANO CHEESE
- 5 pounds fresh RICOTTA CHEESE
- 3 EGGS
- ½ cup chopped fresh PARSLEY
- SALT and PEPPER
- 4 fresh PASTA SHEETS (store-bought), or 2 pounds LASAGNA NOODLES

1. *To make the meatballs:* Soak the bread in the milk. In a medium bowl, mix the ground beef, bread, onions, parsley, eggs, cheese, and garlic. Add salt and pepper to taste. If the mixture is dry, add ½ cup of cold water and mix well. Form into about 12 meatballs.

2. Place the meatballs in a sauté pan with the olive oil and fry over medium to high heat until brown, 10 to 15 minutes. Drain the meatballs on paper towels.

3. In a stockpot, heat the tomato sauce over low heat. Add the meatballs to the sauce and simmer over low heat, covered, for 30 minutes, or until meatballs are cooked through. Remove from the heat and set aside.

4. *To make the lasagna:* Mix ¾ of the mozzarella, 1 cup of the Parmigiano Reggiano, and the ricotta in a large bowl. Add the eggs and parsley. Season with salt and pepper and set aside.

5. Remove the meatballs from the sauce. Crumble the meatballs and set aside.

6. Bring a large pot of salted water to a boil over high heat and cook the pasta until al dente, about 1 minute. Drain and shock in cold water.

7. *To assemble:* Preheat the oven to 350°F. Pour 1 cup of the hot tomato sauce in the bottom of an 8- by 12-inch baking pan. Place a pasta sheet over the layer of sauce, cutting the sheet to fit if necessary.

8. Spread ⅓ of the cheese mixture over the pasta. Spread ⅓ of the crumbled meatballs over the cheese. Add some of the sauce and sprinkle with the remaining ¼ of the mozzarella and Parmesan. Repeat the layers of sauce, pasta, cheese, and meatballs two more times.

9. Spread the remaining cup of tomato sauce over the top layer of the pasta and sprinkle the remaining Parmigiano Reggiano cheese over the sauce.

10. Bake the lasagna for 1 hour, or until the top is golden brown and the sides are bubbling.

ORECCHIETTE WITH ASPARAGUS, SWEET PEAS, AND PROSCIUTTO

6 SERVINGS

This great summer pasta allows you to spend a minimum amount of time over a hot stove.

FOR THE GREEN PEA PUREE

- 1 tablespoon chopped GARLIC
- 1 WHITE ONION, cut in half
- 3 tablespoons OLIVE OIL
- 1 cup DRY WHITE WINE
- 2 cups CHICKEN STOCK (see recipe on page 29)
- 4 cups fresh GREEN PEAS
- SALT and PEPPER

FOR THE PASTA

- 2 pounds uncooked ORECCHIETTE PASTA
- 1 tablespoon chopped SHALLOTS
- 2 tablespoons chopped GARLIC
- 3 cups sliced ASPARAGUS
- 2 tablespoons OLIVE OIL
- 3 cups CHICKEN STOCK
- 1 cup finely julienned PROSCIUTTO
- 3 tablespoons BUTTER
- 1 cup grated PARMESAN CHEESE
- SALT and PEPPER

1. *To make the green pea puree:* In a sauté pan over medium heat, sauté the garlic and onion in the olive oil. Add the white wine and reduce by half. Add the chicken stock and reduce by half again.

2. Add the peas and salt and pepper to taste, and bring to a boil. Puree the mixture in a blender.

3. *To make the pasta:* Bring a pot of salted water to a boil. Cook the pasta for 8 minutes, or until al dente. Drain and set aside.

4. In a sauté pan over medium heat, cook the shallots, garlic, and asparagus in the olive oil until soft, about 4 minutes.

5. Add the chicken stock and cook for about 5 minutes.

6. Add the prosciutto and sauté for 5 minutes, or until wilted.

7. Stir in the butter, pasta, and green pea puree. Add the Parmesan cheese and salt and pepper to taste.

SUNDAY SAUCE WITH MEATBALLS, SAUSAGES, AND PORK CHOPS

6 SERVINGS

This is our traditional sauce that we continue to make at home. Every Sunday, this sauce is cooking on my stove. The aromas take me back to my childhood, when we lived in a three-family house on Union Street in Brooklyn. As you passed each apartment, out came a different aroma. My aunt Mary put raisins in her meatballs; the dish was sweet smelling. My aunt Josie used pigskin to enhance the flavor in her sauce. And by the time I got to the top floor, where I lived, it smelled the best, because my mom made it.

Today my husband, Anthony, cooks the Sunday Sauce. Sometimes it's better than mine. We enjoy doing it for our children and grandchildren. Our family continues to grow—the last count is seventeen.

My grandmother served the meat on a separate platter, but you can add it on top of your pasta. —Marion

- ½ cup EXTRA-VIRGIN OLIVE OIL
- 1 pound MILD SAUSAGE
- ½ pound HOT ITALIAN SAUSAGE
- 6 thinly sliced PORK CHOPS (about 3 pounds)
- 2 cups DRY RED WINE
- 2 tablespoons chopped GARLIC
- 2 ONIONS, diced
- 1 cup diced PANCETTA
- 1 tablespoon crushed RED PEPPER
- 1 gallon canned ITALIAN TOMATOES
- SALT
- 2 cups chopped fresh BASIL
- 2 pounds cooked MEATBALLS (see recipe on page 74)
- 1 pound uncooked RIGATONI

1. In a large pot over medium heat, heat the oil and sauté the sausage and pork chops until brown, about 10 minutes. Don't worry if the meat is not cooked through; it will cook through in the sauce. Remove the meat from the pan and set aside. Deglaze the pan with 1 cup of the red wine.

2. In the same pot, add the garlic, onions, pancetta, and crushed pepper and cook until the onions and garlic are lightly browned, about 2 minutes. Add the remaining cup of red wine and reduce by half. Add the tomatoes and salt to taste and simmer for 1 hour over low heat.

3. Add the basil, sausage, pork chops, and meatballs to the tomato sauce and simmer for an additional hour over low heat.

4. In a large pot of boiling, salted water, cook the pasta for 10 to 12 minutes, or until al dente. Drain the pasta, toss it with the Sunday sauce, and serve immediately.

Total cooking time: 2 hours, 15 minutes.

VEGETABLE LASAGNA

6 SERVINGS

FOR THE BÉCHAMEL

- 4 tablespoons BUTTER
- 2½ tablespoons FLOUR
- 2½ cups WHOLE MILK
- 1 pinch NUTMEG
- 1 SHALLOT, peeled
- SALT

FOR THE LASAGNA

- 1½ pounds ONIONS, diced (about 2 medium ONIONS)
- 8 tablespoons BUTTER
- SALT
- 4 tablespoons OLIVE OIL
- 1½ pounds CARROTS, diced (about 6 medium CARROTS)
- 1 pound SPINACH
- 1½ pounds MOZZARELLA, diced
- 5 pounds fresh RICOTTA CHEESE
- 3 EGGS
- 2 tablespoons chopped fresh PARSLEY
- 1½ cups ARTICHOKES marinated in olive oil, drained and chopped
- BLACK PEPPER
- 2 cups TOMATO SAUCE (see recipe on page 79)
- 4 fresh PASTA SHEETS (store-bought), or 2 pounds LASAGNE NOODLES
- 1 pound roasted RED PEPPERS, julienned (about 2½ large peppers)
- 1 pound PARMIGIANO REGGIANO CHEESE, grated

1. *To make the béchamel:* In a small saucepan over low heat, melt the butter. Stir in the flour to make a paste. This will form a roux. Continue stirring for 2 minutes while it thickens.

2. In a separate saucepan, heat 2 cups of the milk and whisk in the nutmeg and the shallot. Bring to a boil over medium heat and simmer, uncovered, for 3 minutes.

3. Pour the hot milk mixture into the flour and whisk vigorously. Bring to a boil over medium heat, reduce the heat, and simmer for 2 minutes. You want to avoid lumps, and when you see a smooth and thickened texture, season with salt.

4. Strain through a sieve into a bowl and whisk in the remaining ½ cup of milk. Set aside.

5. *To make the lasagna:* In a medium sauté pan over medium heat, sauté the onions in the butter until they soften and begin to caramelize. Season with salt and remove from heat.

6. In another sauté pan over medium heat, heat the olive oil and sauté the carrots until al dente. Add the spinach and continue to sauté for 1 to 2 minutes. Season with salt and drain the liquid from the vegetables.

7. In a mixing bowl, combine the onions, carrots, and spinach. Mix in the mozzarella, ricotta, eggs, parsley, artichokes, and salt and black pepper to taste.

8. Preheat the oven to 350°F. Spread ½ of the tomato sauce in the bottom of a 9- by 13-inch baking pan.

9. Cover the sauce with a pasta sheet (cut sheets to fit if needed), or uncooked fresh lasagna noodles, overlapping slightly.

10. Spread ¼ of the cheese and vegetable mixture over the pasta. Repeat steps 9 and 10 twice.

11. Spread the béchamel and tomato sauce over the top layer of pasta and finish with the remaining Parmigiano Reggiano cheese.

12. Bake the lasagna for 1 hour, or until the top is golden brown and the sides are bubbling.

PENNE WITH FRESH TOMATO SAUCE

6 SERVINGS

- ½ cup EXTRA-VIRGIN OLIVE OIL
- 3 GARLIC CLOVES, minced
- 2 pounds ripe TOMATOES, peeled, seeded, and chopped
- ¼ to 1 teaspoon crushed HOT RED PEPPER flakes
- 1 teaspoon SALT
- 8 fresh BASIL LEAVES, finely shredded
- 1 pound uncooked PENNE PASTA
- 2 tablespoons UNSALTED BUTTER, at room temperature
- Freshly grated PARMIGIANO REGGIANO CHEESE

1. In a large saucepan over medium heat, heat the olive oil. Add the garlic and cook, stirring, for 3 minutes, or until the garlic just begins to turn golden brown. Increase the heat to medium-high, add the tomatoes, red pepper flakes, and salt, and cook, stirring occasionally, for 15 minutes, or until the tomatoes are softened and a sauce is formed. Stir in the basil.

2. Meanwhile, cook the pasta in a large pot of boiling, salted water until al dente, about one minute less than the package directions. Drain the pasta in a colander, reserving 1 cup of the cooking water.

3. Return the pasta to the cooking pot and add the sauce. Add the reserved cooking water and cook, stirring, over medium-high heat for 2 minutes, or until the sauce adheres to the pasta. Stir in the butter.

4. Arrange the pasta in a serving bowl and top with the Parmigiano Reggiano.

CRESPELLE WITH SIX CHEESES

10 SERVINGS

This recipe is rich . . . it will melt in your mouth.

FOR THE CRESPELLE

- 10 EGGS
- 4 cups WHOLE MILK
- 2 cups ALL-PURPOSE FLOUR
- SALT and PEPPER
- OLIVE OIL for cooking

FOR THE CHEESE FILLING

- 2 cups chopped fresh SPINACH, cooked and drained (should equal 1 cup after cooking)
- 1 tablespoon chopped GARLIC
- ½ cup OLIVE OIL
- 1 cup diced MOZZARELLA
- 1 cup diced PROVOLONE
- 1 cup fresh RICOTTA CHEESE
- 1 cup diced BEL PAESE
- 1 cup diced PARMESAN
- 1 cup diced PECORINO ROMANO
- 1 EGG
- SALT and PEPPER

FOR THE ASSEMBLY

- 2 cups BÉCHAMEL SAUCE (see recipe on page 80)
- 2 cups grated PARMESAN CHEESE
- 3 cups TOMATO SAUCE (see recipe on page 79)
- 2 tablespoons BASIL OIL (store-bought)

1. *To make the crespelle:* Whisk all the crespelle ingredients together (except the oil) and pass through a sieve. Chill in refrigerator for 2 to 4 hours.

2. For each crespelle, in a nonstick crepe pan over low heat, add 1 teaspoon of the olive oil and wipe off. Add ¼ cup of the crespelle mixture, coat the entire pan, and cook until the crepe is light golden brown on each side. Keep covered and warm while you cook the remaining crepes and finish the recipe.

3. *To make the cheese mixture:* Sauté the spinach with the chopped garlic in the olive oil; let cool.

4. Mix together the spinach and cheeses. Mix in the egg and salt and pepper to taste.

5. *To assemble:* Preheat the oven to 350°F. Spread ½ cup of the cheese mixture on each crepe and roll them into cylinders. Place all the crepes in one baking pan and top each one with the béchamel, Parmesan cheese, and tomato sauce.

6. Bake for 8 minutes, or until golden brown. Drizzle the serving plate lightly with basil oil. Serve immediately.

Growing up, I was always a thin child. When I reached age ten, I began to acquire a taste for these crespelle. I also began to grow out of my clothes. One day my mom and dad mentioned to me that I seemed to be growing in more places than one. I noticed it myself but tried to justify it by referring to my panty hose chart. On the back of every package there is a weight chart and you could weigh anywhere from 90 pounds to 160 pounds. So I told them, I still weigh less than the panty hose chart, so I must be ahead of the game. My parents had a good laugh.

I continued to eat crespelle . . . but less often.

—Elaina

four

ENTRÉES

SOME OF THESE RECIPES WE GREW UP WITH, AND OTHERS ARE OUR VERSIONS OF WONDERFUL DISHES WE TASTED ON OUR TRAVELS TO FRANCE AND ITALY.

EGGPLANT AND ZUCCHINI PIE

6 SERVINGS

Eggplant and Zucchini Pie was created for Kathie Lee Gifford. Every time she came into the restaurant we made her this special dish, and it became so popular that we put it on our menu. When Live with Regis and Kathie Lee *came to an end, her farewell dinner was given at Fresco and a good time was had by all. We were saddened to see this dynamic duo part company. What a bittersweet moment it was.*

But there is a happy ending to this story . . . we still see Kathie Lee and Regis regularly at Fresco.

—The Scotto Family

FOR THE CHEESE MIXTURE

- 2 pounds fresh RICOTTA CHEESE
- 2 pounds fresh MOZZARELLA CHEESE
- ½ pound PARMESAN CHEESE, grated
- ¼ cup chopped fresh PARSLEY
- 4 EGGS
- SALT and PEPPER

FOR THE EGGPLANT AND ZUCCHINI PIE

- 2 EGGPLANTS, peeled
- 4 ZUCCHINI
- SALT
- 4 cups ALL-PURPOSE FLOUR
- 10 EGGS
- 4 cups dried BREAD CRUMBS (store-bought)
- 1½ cups grated PARMESAN CHEESE
- ¼ cup chopped fresh PARSLEY
- PEPPER
- 2 quarts EXTRA-VIRGIN OLIVE OIL
- 5 cups TOMATO SAUCE (see recipe on page 79
- ½ cup grated PARMESAN CHEESE

1. *To make the cheese mixture:* In a large bowl, combine the ricotta, mozzarella, Parmesan, parsley, and eggs. Mix well and season with salt and pepper to taste. Refrigerate briefly to make the mixture firm.

2. *To make the eggplant and zucchini pie:* Slice the eggplants and zucchini into ¼-inch-thick slices. Set the zucchini aside. Fill a bowl with lightly salted water, add the eggplants, and soak for 1½ to 2 hours to remove the bitter taste.

3. In one shallow bowl, place the flour. In a second bowl, beat the eggs with a fork until blended. In a third bowl, mix the bread crumbs, cheese, parsley, and salt and pepper to taste. Line up the bowls on a work surface.

4. One at a time, carefully dip the eggplant and zucchini slices first into the flour, making sure both sides are covered; then into the egg mixture; and finally into the bread crumb mixture. Coat both sides very well, and gently tap off any excess coating. Transfer to a large plate and season with salt and pepper.

5. In a large, heavy skillet over medium heat, heat the olive oil. Add the eggplant slices and sauté on both sides until golden brown, or about 3 minutes, making sure that they are cooked all the way through and soft. Try not to crowd the pan. Fry the zucchini next. Place the cooked eggplant and zucchini slices on paper towels to drain off the excess oil.

6. Preheat the oven to 450°F. In a 9- by 13-inch baking pan, spread 1 cup of the tomato sauce over the bottom of the pan, then add a layer of ¼ of the eggplant and zucchini slices, and top with ¼ of the cheese mixture Repeat the process three more times. Top with a layer of tomato sauce and sprinkle with the Parmesan cheese.

7. Bake for 20 minutes, or until golden brown. Serve immediately.

ZUPPA DI PESCE

6 SERVINGS

This was our favorite dish in Venice, and as we traveled throughout Italy, we noticed that each region had its own unique way of preparing Zuppa di Pesce.

Last year my daughters-in-law, Theresa and Maria Elena, surprised us by making this recipe for the family. They knew it was my favorite, and it was exceptional. I felt like I was back in Venice!

—Marion

- 1 CARROT, finely diced
- 1 RED ONION, finely diced
- 1 STALK CELERY, finely diced
- 2 LEEKS, cleaned and finely diced
- 1 FENNEL BULB, finely diced
- 1 16-ounce can TOMATOES, with juice
- 4 tablespoons OLIVE OIL
- 1 teaspoon SPICY RED PEPPER flakes
- 1 teaspoon dried OREGANO
- 2 cups DRY WHITE WINE
- 1 16-ounce can CLAM JUICE
- SALT
- 2 tablespoons chopped GARLIC
- 1 1-pound fillet SEA BASS, cut into 4 pieces
- 12 large SHRIMP, peeled and deveined
- 20 MANILA CLAMS (or COCKLES)
- 1 pound CALAMARI, cleaned and cut into slices
- 12 MUSSELS, cleaned
- 4 UNPEELED RED TOMATOES, diced
- 4 UNPEELED YELLOW TOMATOES, diced
- 1 cup cooked CANNELLINI BEANS (canned or fresh)
- 2 tablespoons chopped fresh BASIL

1. In a large sauté pan over medium heat, heat 2 tablespoons of the olive oil. Sauté the carrot, onion, celery, leeks, fennel for 5 minutes. Add the canned tomatoes and cook for 10 minutes. Add the red pepper and oregano.

2. To deglaze the pan, add the wine and stir over medium heat for 10 minutes. Add the clam juice and cook over medium to low heat for 15 to 25 minutes, or until the flavors are melded and the sauce thickens slightly. Add salt to taste.

3. In a large sauté pan over low heat, sauté the garlic in the remaining 2 tablespoons of olive oil for 2 minutes on each side, or until golden brown. Pan-sear the fish for about 5 minutes, turning once, until golden brown on each side. Set the sea bass aside on a plate. Add the shrimp and sauté 1 minute. Add the clams and calamari and sauté 1 minute (the clam shells will not open yet). Add the mussels and sauté 1 minute. Add the reserved sea bass and the sauce and cook 5 to 10 minutes over low heat, or until the clams and mussels open and the soup is the desired consistency. Add extra clam juice if the soup seems too thick.

4. Warm the cannellini beans over low heat. Drain them before serving.

5. Garnish with the diced tomatoes, cannellini beans, and chopped basil.

EGGPLANT-WRAPPED HALIBUT

6 SERVINGS

This dish tastes as good as it looks. It's wonderful for a dinner party.

- 6 ½-pound boneless HALIBUT FILLETS
- SALT and PEPPER
- EXTRA-VIRGIN OLIVE OIL
- 3 to 4 medium EGGPLANTS
- 4 ripe RED TOMATOES, diced
- 4 ripe YELLOW TOMATOES, diced
- 1 tablespoon chopped fresh BASIL
- ½ cup BALSAMIC VINEGAR
- 1 cup BASIL OIL (store-bought)

1. Season the halibut with salt and pepper. In a sauté pan over medium heat, heat 2 tablespoons of olive oil. Sear the fish for about 2 minutes on each side, or until golden brown. Set aside to cool.

2. Slice the eggplants lengthwise to a thickness of about ⅙ inch, or thinner if possible.

3. In a medium bowl, marinate the diced red and yellow tomatoes, basil, salt and pepper to taste, and 4 tablespoons olive oil.

4. Cover the bottom of a large sauté pan with ½ inch of olive oil. Heat over high heat to about 375°F. Fry the eggplant slices until they are soft, or about 30 seconds.

5. Pour the vinegar into a shallow bowl. Drain the eggplant slices on paper towels and then lightly dip them into the vinegar. Place the slices on a plate and set aside.

6. Preheat the oven to 425°F. For each serving, overlap 3 eggplant slices. Place 1 tablespoon of the marinated tomatoes in the center. Place 1 halibut fillet on the tomatoes and wrap tightly with the eggplant. Overlapping makes the package secure. Repeat the process to make a total of 6 eggplant packages.

7. Lay the eggplant packages on a nonstick cookie sheet. Tuck the flaps underneath; this will hold them in place. Bake for 8 to 9 minutes.

8. Top with more of the marinated tomatoes and drizzle with the basil oil. This dish goes well with Sautéed String Beans.

GRILLED SCAMPI WITH VEGETABLE RICE SALAD

6 SERVINGS

This is a great dish for a summer barbecue.

FOR THE RICE SALAD

- ½ cup EXTRA-VIRGIN OLIVE OIL
- 1 tablespoon chopped GARLIC
- 2 tablespoons chopped SHALLOTS
- 2 cups uncooked WHITE RICE
- 4 cups CHICKEN STOCK (see recipe on page 29)
- SALT and BLACK PEPPER

FOR THE PESTO

- ¼ cup PINE NUTS
- 1 tablespoon chopped GARLIC
- ½ cup chopped fresh BASIL
- 1 cup OLIVE OIL
- 2 tablespoons grated PARMESAN CHEESE
- SALT and BLACK PEPPER

FOR THE SCAMPI

- 5 pounds large SHRIMP, shelled and deveined
- SALT and PEPPER
- OLIVE OIL

FOR THE VEGETABLE MIX

- ½ cup chopped ZUCCHINI
- ½ cup chopped SQUASH
- ½ cup chopped CARROT
- ¼ cup chopped FENNEL
- ¼ cup chopped RED ONION
- ¼ cup chopped RED PEPPER
- ¼ cup chopped YELLOW PEPPER
- ¼ cup chopped EGGPLANT
- 1 tablespoon chopped GARLIC
- 2 tablespoons OLIVE OIL
- SALT and BLACK PEPPER

1. *To make the rice salad:* In a medium pot over medium heat, heat the oil and sauté the garlic and shallots until golden brown. Add the rice and chicken stock and simmer for about 20 minutes, covered, until the rice is cooked. Add salt and pepper to taste. Let cool.

2. *To make the scampi:* Season the shrimp with salt, pepper, and olive oil. Cook them on a charcoal grill over medium heat until they turn pink.

3. *To make the vegetable mix:* Combine the vegetables in a bowl. In a large sauté pan over medium heat, sauté garlic in the olive oil for 2 minutes, until golden brown. Add vegetables and cook until tender, about 5 minutes. Add salt and pepper to taste.

4. *To make the pesto:* Preheat the oven to 350°F. Spread the pine nuts on a baking sheet and toast in the oven for 3 minutes, or until golden brown.

5. In a food processor, combine the garlic, basil, olive oil, and toasted pine nuts. Process until mixed and smooth. Add the Parmesan cheese and salt and pepper to taste.

6. In a large bowl, mix the rice, vegetables, and pesto. Transfer to a large platter and place the shrimp in the center.

The cousins' club, 1970.

PEPPERED SALMON WITH PORT WINE VINAIGRETTE

4 SERVINGS

This dish goes wonderfully with Roasted Garlic Mashed Potatoes (see recipe on page 129).

FOR THE SALMON FILLETS

- 4 ½-pound SALMON FILLETS (skin on)
- SEA SALT
- 2 tablespoons BUTTER, melted
- ½ cup coarsely crushed BLACK PEPPER
- 2 tablespoons OLIVE OIL

FOR THE PORT WINE VINAIGRETTE

- 3 EGG YOLKS
- 2 tablespoons DIJON MUSTARD
- SALT and PEPPER
- ½ cup RED WINE VINEGAR
- ½ cup CORN OIL
- ½ cup PORT WINE

1. *To make the salmon fillets:* Season the salmon fillets with sea salt, brush the skin lightly with melted butter, and top the skin with black pepper until covered completely, packing down firmly.

2. Preheat the oven to 350°F. In a large sauté pan over medium heat, heat the olive oil. Place the salmon skin-side down and sear for about 2 minutes, or until pepper adheres. Turn the salmon over into a baking dish, skin-side up, and bake for about 7 minutes, or until done.

3. *To make the port wine vinaigrette:* Place the egg yolks, mustard, salt and pepper to taste, and the vinegar in a food processor. With the machine running, drizzle in a little of the corn oil, then a little of the port wine, alternating until both are incorporated. Serve immediately over the fish.

Note: Raw eggs should not be used in food to be consumed by children, pregnant women, or anyone in poor health or with a compromised immune system because of the danger of salmonella. Make sure you buy the freshest eggs possible.

GRILLED AND BAKED CHILEAN SEA BASS

4 SERVINGS

Jonathan Tisch, who runs Loews Hotels, has been our dear friends for years, and he dines at Fresco often with his family. One evening when he came in for dinner with his two sons, I found the younger son in the kitchen washing our glasses. Shocked, I grabbed him by the hand and sat him at the table with his dad. I told him that his grandfather would be very upset to learn that he was washing my glasses. At that moment his grandfather, Bob Tisch, arrived, and I told him the story. He said that he had started his hotel chain the same way as his grandchild, washing glasses . . . and life goes on!

Jonathan's favorite dish at Fresco is the Chilean Sea Bass.

—Marion

- 4 ½-pound FILLETS CHILEAN SEA BASS
- SALT and PEPPER
- 1 tablespoon OLIVE OIL
- 1 cup DRY WHITE WINE
- 2 tablespoons diced TOMATO
- 2 tablespoons CAPERS
- 1 tablespoon chopped SHALLOTS
- 2 LEMONS, cut into quarters, skinned, and seeded
- 2 tablespoons chopped fresh PARSLEY
- 4 tablespoons BUTTER

1. Preheat the grill to medium heat. Preheat the oven to 375°F.

2. Season the fish fillets with salt and pepper to taste, and brush with the olive oil. Grill briefly on all sides, just until marked enough to give flavor.

3. In a baking pan, add the wine, tomato, capers, shallots, lemon quarters, parsley, and salt and pepper to taste. Place the fillets in a baking pan. Bake for approximately 5 minutes, or until done. Remove the fish from the pan and set aside.

4. Over low heat, add the butter to the pan and whisk into the pan liquids to make a sauce. Pour immediately over the fish and serve.

SEAFOOD CARTOCCIO

4 SERVINGS

We enjoyed this savory recipe in the South of France, where we felt a big connection because of the Italian influence on their cooking. Our first tour guide there was our now-departed friend Lewis Rudin. A few years ago we brought Lew a box of Fresco golf balls for the holidays. That summer Lew hit a hole-in-one at the De Cannes–Mougins golf course with a Fresco golf ball. This ball is now framed on our wall at Fresco and remains a treasured memento of our good friend.

Lew Rudin is missed by all of us! —The Scotto family

- 1 GARLIC CLOVE, chopped
- 1 tablespoon OLIVE OIL
- 2 LEEKS, washed thoroughly and julienned (white part only)
- 1 FENNEL BULB, julienned
- 1 CARROT, julienned
- ¼ cup DRY WHITE WINE
- Pinch of SAFFRON
- SALT and PEPPER
- 1 sprig DILL
- PARCHMENT PAPER
- 1 pound CALAMARI, cut into rings
- 1½ pounds CHILEAN SEA BASS, cut into three ½-pound pieces
- 4 whole SEA SCALLOPS
- 4 large SHRIMP, peeled and deveined
- 20 MANILA CLAMS, cleaned
- 12 NEW ZEALAND MUSSELS, cleaned
- 16 CHERRY TOMATOES, halved
- ½ cup fresh BASIL, julienned
- 1 cup TOMATO SAUCE (see recipe on page 79)
- 2 EGG WHITES, beaten

1. In a large sauté pan over medium heat, sauté the garlic in the olive oil. Add the leeks first, then the fennel and carrots. Sauté for 3 minutes, until the vegetables are cooked but still crunchy. Deglaze with the wine and saffron, then add salt and pepper to taste and the dill.

2. Cut two 12-inch disks from the parchment paper and lay 1 of the disks on a plate. Place the sautéed vegetables and a tablespoon of the cooking juice on the parchment. Add the calamari, sea bass, scallops, and shrimp. Top with the clams and mussels. Add the cherry tomatoes, basil, salt and pepper to taste, and tomato sauce.

3. Preheat the oven to 400°F. Brush the egg whites along the edge of the parchment disk, then top the cartoccio with the second disk and press the edges of the disks together to seal. Bake for 14 minutes, or until cooked.

4. Place on a platter and cut open the parchment with a sharp knife. Serve immediately.

CRAB CAKES WITH AVOCADO SALSA

4 TO 6 SERVINGS

Our customers can't get enough of our crab cakes. I just think they're delicious! —Rosanna

FOR THE AVOCADO SALSA

- 2 large ripe AVOCADOS, peeled
- 1 small ripe TOMATO, diced
- ½ small RED ONION, finely diced
- ¼ cup fresh CORN, cooked
- ¼ cup fresh PEAS, cooked
- ¼ cup finely chopped fresh BASIL
- Juice of 2 LIMES
- 2 tablespoons EXTRA-VIRGIN OLIVE OIL
- TABASCO
- SALT

FOR THE CRAB CAKES

- 1 medium ZUCCHINI, seeds removed, finely chopped, and squeezed dry
- 2 stalks CELERY, finely chopped and squeezed dry
- 2 tablespoons CAPERS, rinsed, finely chopped, and squeezed dry
- 1 large SHALLOT, finely minced
- ½ cup KETCHUP
- ½ cup HELLMANN'S MAYONNAISE
- TABASCO
- 1 pound jumbo lump CRABMEAT, picked clean
- ½ pound dried BREAD CRUMBS
- ½ cup sliced blanched ALMONDS
- ½ cup EXTRA-VIRGIN OLIVE OIL

POTATO CHIPS for garnish

1. *To make the avocado salsa:* In a large bowl, coarsely smash the avocados. Add the rest of the ingredients and mix thoroughly. Adjust the seasonings to taste. Set aside.

2. *To make the crab cakes:* In a large bowl, mix the zucchini, celery, capers, shallot, ketchup, mayonnaise, and Tabasco to taste to make a dressing. Reserve ¼ cup to garnish the crab cakes before serving.

3. Gently fold the dressing into the cleaned crabmeat. Form the crab mixture into 4 balls using a ½-cup measure.

4. Mix the bread crumbs and almonds in a bowl. Thoroughly coat the crab balls in the mixture. Flatten the crab balls to look like hockey pucks.

5. Preheat the oven to 400°F. In a large sauté pan over medium heat, pan-sear the crab cakes in the oil until golden brown, about 3 minutes.

6. Place the crab cakes on a baking sheet and bake for 5 to 6 minutes, or until cooked.

7. To serve, place a generous spoonful of avocado salsa on each plate. Place a crab cake on the avocado salsa. Top with a small spoonful of reserved dressing from step 2. Garnish with potato chips.

PISTACHIO-CRUSTED COD WITH SAFFRON VINAIGRETTE AND RED BLISS POTATOES

6 SERVINGS

We like to make this special dish in the summer, when we're in the mood for something light and tasty.

FOR THE BASIL OIL

- 1 cup chopped fresh BASIL
- 1 cup EXTRA-VIRGIN OLIVE OIL

FOR THE CHERRY TOMATOES

- 2 dozen CHERRY TOMATOES
- 1 teaspoon finely chopped GARLIC
- ½ cup EXTRA-VIRGIN OLIVE OIL
- 1 tablespoon chopped fresh BASIL
- SALT and PEPPER

FOR THE POTATOES

- ½ cup OLIVE OIL
- 1 teaspoon chopped GARLIC
- 3 pounds RED BLISS POTATOES, sliced thin
- 2 tablespoons BUTTER
- ½ cup CHICKEN STOCK (see recipe on page 29)
- 1 tablespoon FENNEL SEEDS
- SALT and PEPPER

1. *To make the basil oil:* Combine the basil and olive oil in a blender and blend on high speed for 1 or 2 minutes, or until smooth. Set aside.

2. *To make the cherry tomatoes:* In a medium saucepan of boiling water, blanch the cherry tomatoes for 10 seconds. Shock in a bowl of ice water. When the tomatoes are cold, drain them and peel off the skins.

3. In a small saucepan over low heat, sauté the garlic in the olive oil. Heat until sizzling and remove from the heat.

4. When the oil and garlic mixture is cooled, add the basil and tomatoes. Season with salt and pepper and set aside.

5. *To make the potatoes:* Preheat the oven to 425°F. In a sauté pan over medium heat, heat the olive oil and add the garlic. When the garlic begins to brown, quickly add the sliced potatoes and stir well. Allow the potatoes to color slightly, about 3 minutes. Add the butter, chicken stock, and fennel seeds. Stir well and season with salt and pepper.

6. Put the potato mixture in a baking dish, cover, and bake for 15 to 18 minutes, or until cooked. Remove from the oven and set aside. Leave the oven on.

7. *To make the saffron vinaigrette:* In a small saucepan over medium heat, combine the wine, shallots, saffron, and squash. Simmer for 5 minutes, or until the vegetables are soft. Remove from the heat.

FOR THE SAFFRON VINAIGRETTE

½ cup DRY WHITE WINE

3 large SHALLOTS, peeled and sliced

1 heaping tablespoon SAFFRON

1 small YELLOW SQUASH, sliced

¼ cup WHITE WINE VINEGAR

1 cup EXTRA-VIRGIN OLIVE OIL

SALT and PEPPER

FOR THE COD

6 ½-pound COD FILLETS

SALT and PEPPER

2 tablespoons whole-grain POMMERY MUSTARD

1 cup finely chopped PISTACHIOS

8. In a blender, puree the saffron mixture. Slowly pour in the white wine vinegar and then add the olive oil and process until emulsified. Season with salt and pepper.

9. *To make the cod:* Season the fish with salt and pepper. Brush one side of each fillet with the mustard, then lightly coat that side with pistachios. Lay the fillets on a baking sheet, coated side up, and bake for 6 to 7 minutes, or until golden brown.

10. For each serving, place some of the potatoes in the center of the plate and top with a fillet of cod. Surround the potatoes with 4 cherry tomatoes. Drizzle the tomatoes with basil oil and garnish the cod with saffron vinaigrette.

ARCTIC CHAR WITH PESTO

6 SERVINGS

To keep the basil pesto green when blending, add some ice cubes. We love pesto on just about anything (except maybe cheesecake).

FOR THE PESTO CRUST

1 cup EXTRA-VIRGIN OLIVE OIL

1 tablespoon chopped GARLIC

1 pound fresh BASIL

½ cup PINE NUTS

1 cup grated PARMESAN CHEESE

¼ cup toasted BREAD CRUMBS (store-bought)

SALT and PEPPER

FOR THE ARCTIC CHAR

1 tablespoon EXTRA-VIRGIN OLIVE OIL

6 ½-pound FILLETS ARCTIC CHAR

6 cups SICILIAN COUSCOUS (see recipe on page 126)

6 teaspoons BASIL OIL (see recipe on page 100)

1. *To make the pesto crust:* In a blender, combine the olive oil, garlic, basil, and pine nuts. Process until mixed. Add the Parmesan cheese and mix.

2. Transfer to a bowl and mix in the bread crumbs and salt and pepper to taste.

3. *To make the arctic char:* In a large sauté pan over high heat, heat the olive oil. Pan-sauté the arctic char until lightly browned on one side, about 2 minutes. Don't cook the other side.

4. Let the fillets cool in the pan for 15 minutes and then coat their uncooked side with the pesto crust.

5. Preheat the oven to 350°F and heat the couscous for 5 minutes.

6. Place the arctic char in the broiler for 6 minutes, or until brown.

7. Transfer the fillets to a serving platter, surround them with the couscous, and garnish each one with a drizzle of basil oil. Serve immediately.

SEARED MONKFISH

4 SERVINGS

Monkfish is sometimes called the poor man's lobster, but there's nothing second-rate about this fish—it's just wonderful!

FOR THE MONKFISH

- 2 pounds MONKFISH FILLETS, cleaned and trimmed of fat
- 1 cup ALL-PURPOSE FLOUR
- 1 tablespoon PAPRIKA
- SALT and PEPPER
- 2 tablespoons EXTRA-VIRGIN OLIVE OIL

FOR THE WHITE WINE SAUCE

- 1 SHALLOT, minced
- 1 cup DRY WHITE WINE
- 1 tablespoon BUTTER

1. *To make the monkfish:* Slice the monkfish on the bias into 2-ounce medallions, about ½ inch thick.

2. In a small bowl, mix the flour and paprika. Season the monkfish medallions with salt and pepper to taste and then thoroughly dust them with the seasoned flour.

3. In a large sauté pan over medium heat, heat the olive oil. When it begins to smoke lightly, add the monkfish medallions (about 3 at a time; avoid crowding the pan). Cook for 1 to 2 minutes on each side, or until golden brown. Remove from the pan and reserve the liquid for the final sauce.

4. *To make the white wine sauce:* Place the minced shallot in the monkfish pan and cook lightly 1 to 2 minutes over medium heat. Add the white wine and bring to a boil over medium to high heat. Reduce by half. Add the cooking liquid from the monkfish. Reduce by half. Remove from the heat.

5. Whisk in the butter to get a thick consistency. Strain and serve over the fish.

CHICKEN CACCIATORE

6 SERVINGS

This classic dish has been passed down for generations in our family. It is one of our favorites. My family was in the poultry business for many years, so my grandmother and mom excelled in preparing chicken. During the lean years, and the best years, chicken was always on our menu. —Marion

- 1 whole 3-pound CHICKEN
- ½ cup ALL-PURPOSE FLOUR
- SALT and PEPPER
- ¾ cup OLIVE OIL
- 1 tablespoon chopped GARLIC
- 1 cup chopped ONION
- 1 cup halved BUTTON MUSHROOMS
- 2 cups diced RED and YELLOW PEPPERS
- ½ cup KALAMATA OLIVES, whole and pitted
- ¼ cup RED WINE VINEGAR
- 2 cups TOMATO SAUCE (see recipe on page 79)
- 1 cup CHICKEN or VEAL STOCK (see recipes on page 29)
- ½ bunch fresh BASIL, chopped fine

1. Cut the chicken into 8 pieces, leaving the bones in and the skin on.

2. Season the flour with salt and pepper to taste. Lightly dust the chicken pieces.

3. In a large sauté pan over medium heat, pan-sear the chicken on all sides in ¼ cup of the olive oil until golden brown, or about 4 minutes. Set aside.

4. In the same pan, heat the remaining ½ cup olive oil and sauté the garlic and onion until light brown, or about 2 minutes.

5. Add the mushrooms, peppers, and kalamata olives and sauté for 5 minutes, or until soft. Deglaze with the red wine vinegar.

6. Add the tomato sauce and stock and simmer over low heat for 5 minutes. Add the chicken and cook for about 30 minutes, or until cooked through. Add the basil and season with salt and pepper to taste.

Marion's mother *(at right)* with her girlfriends in the 1930s.

FRESCO CHICKEN MILANESE WITH CHEESE

6 SERVINGS

You can serve this with or without the cheese; either way is equally delicious. My son, Danny, and daughter, Julia, beg me to make it every week. —*Elaina*

FOR THE CHICKEN CUTLETS

2 cups ALL-PURPOSE FLOUR

6 EGGS

3 cups seasoned dried BREAD CRUMBS (store-bought)

¾ cup grated PARMESAN CHEESE

¼ cup chopped fresh PARSLEY

SALT and PEPPER

6 ½-pound boneless CHICKEN CUTLETS, pounded thin and round

2 cups EXTRA-VIRGIN OLIVE OIL

FOR THE CHEESE MIXTURE

1 pound fresh RICOTTA CHEESE

½ pound fresh MOZZARELLA CHEESE, diced

¼ cup grated PARMESAN CHEESE

1 cup chopped fresh PARSLEY

2 EGGS

SALT and PEPPER

FOR THE RED AND YELLOW TOMATO FLORETS

4 large RED BEEFSTEAK TOMATOES

4 large YELLOW BEEFSTEAK TOMATOES

2 tablespoons dried OREGANO

SALT and PEPPER

1 pound fresh MOZZARELLA, sliced thin

¼ cup julienned fresh BASIL

1. *To make the chicken cutlets:* Put the flour in a shallow bowl. In another bowl, beat the eggs with a fork until they are blended. In a third bowl, mix together the bread crumbs, cheese, parsley, and salt and pepper to taste. Arrange the bowls on a work surface so that they are lined up next to one another.

2. Carefully dip a cutlet into the flour, making sure both sides are covered, dip into the egg mixture, and finally dip into the bread crumb mixture and coat both sides very well while gently tapping off any excess.

3. Transfer to a serving plate, season with salt and pepper, and set aside while repeating with the remaining cutlets.

4. In a large heavy skillet, heat the olive oil over medium heat. Add the cutlets and sauté on both sides until golden brown and cooked through, about 6 minutes. Remove from the pan and place on paper towels to drain the excess oil.

5. *To make the cheese mixture:* In a bowl, mix the ricotta, mozzarella, Parmesan, parsley, and eggs. Mix well and season with salt and pepper to taste. Refrigerate briefly, covered, to make the mixture firm.

6. *To make the red and yellow tomato florets:* Cut the tomatoes in half and then into wedges. Season with the dried oregano and salt and pepper to taste.

7. Preheat the oven to 375°F. On a cookie sheet, place a scoop (3 to 4 tablespoons) of the ricotta cheese mixture in the center of each cutlet and surround with alternating red and yellow tomato wedges (about 6 total), add 2 slices of mozzarella cheese to each cutlet. Season with salt and pepper to taste.

8. Bake for 6 to 8 minutes, or until the cheese is melted. Sprinkle with the fresh basil and serve immediately.

ROAST BABY CHICKEN WITH LEMON AND BASIL

6 SERVINGS

This is a very simple dish to prepare for a quick dinner. Nobody cooked chicken better than my mom. Years ago, people wore their family crest attached to their jackets. The joke among my cousins was that our family crest was a chicken! —Marion

- 6 LEMONS, cut into thin slices
- 1 tablespoon chopped GARLIC
- 1 bunch fresh BASIL, chopped
- SALT and PEPPER
- 6 1½-pound BABY CHICKENS (CORNISH HENS)
- 2 tablespoons BUTTER

1. Preheat the oven to 350°F. In a small bowl, mix the lemon slices, garlic, basil, and salt and pepper to taste.

2. Place the seasoning under the skin of the chickens. Melt the butter and rub it on the outside and inside of the chickens. Season with salt and pepper.

3. Roast the chickens for 30 minutes, or until they are golden brown and their juices run clear.

GRANDMA'S BONELESS STUFFED CHICKEN

6 SERVINGS

This recipe was passed down from my grandmother to my mom. I remember, many years ago, my mom sitting for hours removing the bones from the chickens and then stuffing them. Today we're lucky because we can have a butcher do it for us. I like to serve my stuffed chicken on special occasions. This is our roast beef! —*Marion*

- 1 10-pound ROASTER (CHICKEN) or CAPON
- ¼ cup OLIVE OIL
- ½ cup finely diced ONION
- 2 tablespoons chopped GARLIC
- 1 pound ground SAUSAGE MEAT
- 1 pound ground BEEF
- 1 pound ground VEAL
- 1 pound uncooked RICE (2½ cups)
- 2 pounds MOZZARELLA CHEESE, diced
- ½ cup grated PARMESAN CHEESE
- SALT and PEPPER
- 2 ONIONS, sliced thin
- 2 cups BUTTER, melted
- 1½ cups CHICKEN STOCK (see recipe on page 29)

1. Have the butcher debone the large chicken or capon into a French cut. Pound the chicken to a thickness of about ¼ inch and set aside in the refrigerator.

2. In a sauté pan over medium heat, heat the oil and sauté the onion and garlic until translucent, about 3 minutes. Add the sausage and sauté until lightly brown, then add the beef and veal and sauté until lightly brown. Drain the oil. Transfer the meat to a baking sheet and cool in the refrigerator for a half hour.

3. Cook the rice according to the package instructions. Drain and set aside.

4. In a large mixing bowl, mix the mozzarella, Parmesan, cooked meats, rice, and salt and pepper to taste.

5. Remove the chicken from the refrigerator and place it on a large cutting board. Lay the chicken flat, skin-side down, and season with salt and pepper.

6. Place the meat and cheese mixture in the center of the chicken and roll the chicken into a cylinder lengthwise, making sure that the stuffing remains in the center.

7. Using some butcher twine, tie the two ends first to close off the cylinder, and then wrap the twine around the rest of the chicken.

8. Preheat the oven to 350°F. Place the sliced onions on the bottom of a large roasting pan, top with ½ cup of the butter, and pour in the chicken stock. Place the chicken in the pan, top with the remaining 1½ cups butter, and roast, uncovered, for 35 to 45 minutes, or until golden brown, basting every 10 minutes.

9. Remove from the oven and let rest for 10 minutes. Slice into ¼-inch-thick pieces, arrange on a platter with the braised onions, and pour 1 cup of the pan liquid over the chicken.

The sacred grandmother: Marion's grandmother, Elena, with her son Philip, 1934.

GRILLED MARINATED PORK RIBS

4 SERVINGS

This is a great recipe that doesn't keep you in front of a hot grill for hours and hours.

My sons-in-law, Lou Ruggiero and Dan Faucetta, are always in charge of grilling in the summer. Lou and Dan are attorneys by day and culinary wizards by night. They make the best ribs in town; the ribs are finger-licking good! —*Marion*

- 1 quart WATER
- 1½ cups unsulfured MOLASSES
- 5 GARLIC cloves
- 5 BAY LEAVES
- 2 cups finely sliced ONIONS
- 1½ cups APPLE CIDER
- SALT
- 3 BABY BACK PORK RIBS (about 4 pounds)

1. In a large pot, combine the water, molasses, garlic, bay leaves, onions, apple cider, and salt. Bring the mixture to a boil, remove from the fire, and allow to cool.

2. In a large bowl, marinate the ribs in the mixture for 2 hours, covered, in the refrigerator.

3. Preheat the oven to 350°F. Braise the ribs in the marinade, covered, for 45 minutes to 1 hour, or until cooked.

4. Grill the ribs over medium heat for 10 minutes, or until brown. Serve immediately.

BRAISED LAMB SHANKS WITH ORANGE GREMOLATA

6 SERVINGS

I was having dinner at Fresco with New York Post *columnist Cindy Adams and WNBC-TV anchor Sue Simmons when who should walk in but Bryant Gumbel and his girlfriend, Hillary. They sat down next to us, and Bryant started to tease us about how much food was on the table. Bryant, Hillary, and Cindy became fast friends, even setting a play date for their dogs. Who would have thought that braised lamb shank could bring people together? —Rosanna*

FOR THE BRAISED LAMB SHANKS

½ pound PANCETTA, cooked and diced

6 tablespoons EXTRA-VIRGIN OLIVE OIL

1 large ONION, chopped finely

½ pound CARROTS, chopped finely (about 2 medium carrots)

1 FENNEL BULB, chopped finely

3 tablespoons minced GARLIC

6 pounds LAMB SHANKS

SALT and PEPPER

2 cups DRY RED WINE

3 cups VEAL STOCK (see recipe on page 29)

2 tablespoons chopped fresh THYME

3 cups TOMATO PUREE

Zest of 1 ORANGE and 1 LEMON

FOR THE ORANGE GREMOLATA

2 ORANGES

1 tablespoon chopped fresh PARSLEY

1 tablespoon chopped GARLIC

2 tablespoons EXTRA-VIRGIN OLIVE OIL

1. *To make the braised lamb shanks:* In a nonstick pan over medium heat, cook the pancetta just until the fat is rendered, about 2 minutes. Set aside.

2. In a large saucepan over medium heat, heat 2 tablespoons of the oil. Add the onion, carrots, fennel, and garlic. Cook very slowly, stirring constantly until very soft, 3 to 5 minutes. Transfer the vegetables to a roasting pan large enough to hold the lamb shanks in a single layer.

3. Preheat the oven to 350°F. Season the shanks with salt and pepper. In a large sauté pan over high heat, heat 3 tablespoons oil until very hot. Sear the shanks for about 3 minutes, or until they are nicely browned, turning to brown all sides. Transfer the shanks to the roasting pan. Add the pancetta, red wine, veal stock, thyme, tomato puree, and zests. Cover the pan with foil and roast for 2 hours, or until the meat is tender. Use the liquid on the bottom of the pan for the sauce.

4. *To make the orange gremolata:* Remove the zest from the oranges and mince. Then peel the oranges. Remove the membranes from the orange segments, and place the segments in a bowl. Add the parsley, orange zest, garlic, and olive oil. Mix well.

5. Serve the shanks topped with the orange gremolata, accompanied by Roasted Winter Vegetables (see recipe on page 138).

HERB-CRUSTED BABY RACK OF LAMB

4 SERVINGS

Baby rack of lamb has become so popular that it's one of our signature dishes at Fresco. My son, Anthony III, and daughter, Gabriella, adore this dish. Most times, one rack is not enough!
—Anthony

- ½ pound fresh BREAD CRUMBS
- ¼ cup mixed, finely chopped FRESH HERBS (THYME, ROSEMARY, SAGE, and PARSLEY)
- 2 tablespoons chopped GARLIC
- ½ cup EXTRA-VIRGIN OLIVE OIL
- 4 pounds whole BABY RACK OF LAMB
- ¼ cup DIJON MUSTARD

1. Preheat the oven to 450°F. In a bowl, combine the bread crumbs with the chopped herbs. Add the garlic and oil and blend thoroughly.

2. Heat a large sauté pan over high heat and sear the rack of lamb until dark brown, about 4 minutes. Allow it to cool for a minute. Brush the lamb with the mustard and then roll the lamb in the bread crumbs to cover.

3. Place the rack of lamb in the roasting pan and cook for approximately 12 minutes, or until it is medium rare.

GRILLED LAMB CHOPS MARINATED IN HONEY MUSTARD

8 SERVINGS

- ½ cup EXTRA-VIRGIN OLIVE OIL
- 2 RED ONIONS, julienned
- ¼ cup SUGAR
- 2 cups DRY RED WINE
- 2 cups RED WINE VINEGAR
- ½ cup HONEY
- 1 cup DIJON MUSTARD
- 4 RACKS OF LAMB, cut into chops (6 pounds)
- SALT and PEPPER

1. In a large sauté pan over low heat, heat the olive oil. Add the onions and sauté for 2 minutes, or until golden brown. Add the sugar, wine, and red wine vinegar. Cook for an additional 3 minutes, or until hot. Set aside at room temperature.

2. When the mixture is cool, transfer to a medium bowl and add the honey and mustard. Mix well. Marinate the racks of lamb in the mixture overnight, covered, in the refrigerator.

3. Remove the chops from the marinade. Heat the grill to medium heat, sprinkle the chops with salt and pepper, and grill for a few minutes on each side, or until cooked to the desired degree of doneness. Serve hot.

VEAL MILANESE

4 SERVINGS

This is a great summer dish. It can be cooked ahead of time and served at room temperature.

We prepared this recipe for our first appearance on NBC's Today *show. We all knew how important this could be for Fresco. Rosanna prepared us with questions and timed us continuously for the segment. When it was showtime, Matt Lauer asked the opening question: "What is Tuscan food?"*

At that moment, I froze*! No words came out of my mouth . . . I even forgot that I was Italian, never mind what Tuscan food is!*

But our NBC family—Katie Couric, Al Roker, Ann Curry, and Matt Lauer—was so nice to me and my family that I regained my composure and we went on with the show. —Marion

FOR THE VEAL

- 3 EGGS
- ½ cup ALL-PURPOSE FLOUR
- 2 cups HERB BREAD CRUMBS (a mix of ROSEMARY, THYME, and SAGE, or store-bought)
- ¼ cup grated PARMESAN CHEESE
- 4 ¾-pound VEAL CHOPS, butterflied and pounded
- 1 cup OLIVE OIL

FOR THE GARNISH

- 1 pound ARUGULA, torn
- 1 RED TOMATO, diced
- 1 YELLOW TOMATO, diced
- ¼ cup julienned fresh BASIL
- ¾ cup cooked CANNELLINI BEANS (canned or homemade)
- Juice of 2 LEMONS
- ½ cup EXTRA-VIRGIN OLIVE OIL
- SALT and PEPPER

1. *To make the veal:* In a shallow dish, whisk the eggs. In a second dish, put the flour. In a third shallow dish, combine the bread crumbs and Parmesan cheese. Lightly flour the veal, dip the floured veal into the eggs, and toss the egg-coated veal in the bread crumb–Parmesan cheese mixture.

2. In a sauté pan over medium heat, sauté the veal in the olive oil until golden brown on the outside (medium rare), or about 5 minutes on each side.

3. *To make the garnish:* In a bowl, mix the arugula, red and yellow tomatoes, basil, beans, lemon juice, and olive oil. Add salt and pepper to taste. Place a veal chop on each serving plate and top with a portion of the arugula salad.

VEAL OSSO BUCO

6 SERVINGS

This hearty winter dish warms the heart and soothes the soul.

- ¼ cup dried PORCINI MUSHROOMS
- ¼ cup plus 2 tablespoons OLIVE OIL
- 6 1½-inch-thick VEAL SHANKS
- ¼ pound PANCETTA, chopped into small pieces
- 1 cup finely chopped CARROTS (about 4 CARROTS)
- 1 cup finely chopped FENNEL BULB
- 1 cup finely chopped ONIONS (about 2 large ONIONS)
- 2 tablespoons chopped GARLIC
- 1 RED PEPPER, chopped
- 1 tablespoon chopped fresh ROSEMARY
- 1 cup DRY RED WINE
- 2 cups VEAL STOCK (see recipe on page 29) or BEEF STOCK
- 1 cup canned PUREED TOMATOES
- ½ pound OYSTER MUSHROOMS, sliced
- ½ pound SHIITAKE MUSHROOMS, sliced
- SALT and PEPPER

1. Soak the dried porcini mushrooms in hot water for 20 minutes, or until soft. Remove the mushrooms, reserve the liquid, and finely chop the mushrooms.

2. In a large sauté pan over medium heat, heat ¼ cup of the olive oil until very hot. Brown the shanks, about 3 minutes on each side, cooking 2 to 3 at a time, depending on the size of the pan. Remove the shanks to a plate.

3. Drain the grease from the pan and put the heat on low. Add the pancetta and cook until the fat is rendered and the meat starts to brown, 10 to 12 minutes. Add the carrots, fennel, onions, garlic, red pepper, and rosemary to the pan and cook over low heat for 30 minutes, until the vegetables are soft and any liquid has evaporated. Add the wine, stock, porcini mushrooms, strained reserved mushroom liquid, and tomatoes and bring to a boil over high heat.

4. Preheat the oven to 350°F. Place the shanks in a large roasting pan and pour the vegetable mixture over them, moving the shanks to let some cooking liquid under them. Braise, covered, for 2 hours, or until the shanks are very tender.

5. When the shanks are almost done, in a large sauté pan over medium heat, sauté the fresh mushrooms in the remaining 2 tablespoons of olive oil for 5 to 6 minutes, or until they have wilted and released their moisture. Remove from the pan and let cool.

6. Remove the cooked shanks to a platter and keep them warm in the oven. Place the braising liquid and the vegetables, in a small saucepan and reduce to about 3 cups. Season with salt and pepper if needed, add the mushrooms, and heat through. Serve the shanks topped with the mushroom sauce.

When Hillary Clinton was first lady, she attended a fund-raiser at Fresco. Her advance people came the day before and told Anthony Jr. that she would probably come in the employees' entrance and that we should be prepared for her to use the employees' bathroom. This is not the most luxurious bathroom in the restaurant, so for twenty-four hours we killed ourselves repainting, hanging mirrors, and framing pictures. We also got a new, cushiony toilet seat.

When Mrs. Clinton arrived, Anthony Jr., Rosanna, Elaina, and I greeted her. We mentioned to her that the ladies' room was available. She smiled but didn't answer. I again said to Mrs. Clinton, "This is the way to the powder room." Her secret service agent grabbed my hand and said, "Mrs. Clinton doesn't need to use the bathroom." To this day, we affectionately call the room Hillary's Throne.

We sent a few portions of our Veal Osso Buco back to Washington aboard *Air Force One.*

—*Marion*

PORCINI-CRUSTED LOIN OF VEAL WITH PORCINI MUSHROOM SAUCE

6 SERVINGS

Grinding up dried mushrooms to coat a piece of meat may sound crazy, but the result is mouthwatering.

We first had this dish in Monaco with my father-in-law, Peter Faucetta. He took the entire family to a wonderful restaurant in a charming village called Eze. We call Peter "Mr. Monaco" because he knows every great restaurant, hotel, and village to visit. A trip to Europe would not be complete without our Peter! —Elaina

FOR THE VEAL

- 2 cups dried PORCINI MUSHROOMS, finely ground in a blender
- SALT and PEPPER
- 2 pounds VEAL TENDERLOIN, cut into 6 medallions
- 2 tablespoons OLIVE OIL

FOR THE PORCINI SAUCE

- ½ cup OLIVE OIL
- 2 tablespoons chopped SHALLOTS
- 1 tablespoon chopped GARLIC
- ½ pound fresh (or frozen) PORCINI MUSHROOMS, diced
- 1 sprig fresh THYME, leaves only
- 1 cup DRY WHITE WINE
- 1 cup VEAL STOCK (see recipe on page 29)
- 1 tablespoon BUTTER
- SALT and PEPPER

1. *To make the veal:* In a small bowl, mix the ground mushrooms, and salt and pepper to taste. Rub the mixture into the medallions, coating thoroughly.

2. Preheat the oven to 450°F. In a medium sauté pan over medium heat, heat the olive oil. Add the veal medallions and pan-sear until light brown on each side, about 3 minutes.

3. Lay the medallions on a baking sheet and bake for about 7 minutes, or until cooked. Set aside and keep covered.

4. *To make the porcini sauce:* In a medium sauté pan over medium heat, heat ¼ cup of the olive oil, add the shallots and garlic, and sauté lightly for 2 minutes, or until golden brown. Add the mushrooms and brown lightly, about 2 minutes. Add the thyme.

5. Deglaze with the white wine and cook over medium heat for 10 minutes, or until reduced by half. Add the veal stock and reduce by half again. Stir in butter and remaining olive oil. Add salt and pepper to taste.

6. Slice, present on a platter, and top with porcini mushroom sauce.

VEAL SCALOPPINI WITH TOMATO, BASIL, MOZZARELLA, AND ROASTED POTATOES

6 SERVINGS

FOR THE ROASTED POTATOES

2 pounds very small new POTATOES

2 tablespoons OLIVE OIL

7 cloves GARLIC, peeled

2 large sprigs ROSEMARY, leaves only

SALT and PEPPER

FOR THE VEAL

12 3-ounce MEDALLIONS VEAL SCALLOPINI

SALT and PEPPER

¼ cup OLIVE OIL

½ cup finely chopped fresh BASIL

2 large ripe TOMATOES, cut into 12 slices total

1 pound fresh salted MOZZARELLA, cut into 12 slices

1 teaspoon dried OREGANO

1. *To make the roasted potatoes:* Preheat the oven to 350°F. In a bowl, toss the potatoes, olive oil, garlic, and rosemary. Sprinkle with salt and pepper.

2. Place on a baking sheet and roast for 12 to 15 minutes.

3. *To make veal:* While potatoes are cooking, season the veal scaloppini with salt and pepper.

4. In a large nonstick skillet over medium heat, add the oil. When it begins to smoke lightly, pan-sear the veal a few pieces at a time, until light brown on each side, about 2 minutes per side. As each piece is done, remove it from the pan and drain it on a paper towel.

5. Preheat the oven to 425°F. Place the pieces of veal on a separate baking sheet. Top each piece with the basil, tomato, mozzarella, and oregano.

6. Bake for 2 to 3 minutes, or until the mozzarella begins to melt.

7. Place potatoes first, then veal on top of each plate. Serve hot.

GRILLED FILET MIGNON FOR TWO

2 SERVINGS

Stir up some romance by serving this dish on Valentine's Day. It doesn't take very long to cook, which leaves you with the rest of the evening to spend with your loved one.

FOR THE BEEF

- 1 pound BEEF TENDERLOIN (FILET MIGNON)
- SALT and PEPPER
- EXTRA-VIRGIN OLIVE OIL

FOR THE BAROLO SAUCE

- 1 tablespoon chopped SHALLOTS
- 1 tablespoon chopped GARLIC
- 2 tablespoons EXTRA-VIRGIN OLIVE OIL
- 4 cups DRY RED WINE, barolo preferred
- 2 cups VEAL STOCK (see recipe on page 29)
- 4 tablespoons BUTTER, melted
- 1 teaspoon chopped fresh ROSEMARY
- SALT and PEPPER

1. *To make the beef:* Season the beef tenderloin with salt and pepper. Brush with olive oil and grill over medium heat to medium rare, or approximately 14 minutes.

2. *To make the barolo sauce:* In a medium sauté pan, sauté the shallots and garlic in the olive oil until golden, about 2 minutes. Deglaze with the wine, add the veal stock, and reduce by half until the texture is syrupy. Whisk in the butter slowly, add the chopped rosemary, and season with salt and pepper. Carve the beef and serve immediately with the sauce.

five

SIDES

THESE ARE JUST A HANDFUL OF OUR FAVORITE SIDE DISHES. WHILE YOU'RE COOKING, DON'T HESITATE TO SUBSTITUTE SOME OF YOUR OWN FAVORITE VEGETABLES. DEPENDING UPON THE SEASON AND WHAT THE MARKET HAS TO OFFER, YOU CAN BE CREATIVE AND IMAGINATIVE BY USING THE FRESHEST INGREDIENTS.

SEASONAL MUSHROOMS

6 SERVINGS

These mushrooms are full of flavor—an excellent choice to serve with Grilled Filet Mignon for Two (see recipe on page 122).

- 1½ pounds assorted SEASONAL MUSHROOMS (CRIMINI, SHIITAKE, and/or OYSTER)
- 1 clove GARLIC, peeled and chopped
- 2 SHALLOTS, peeled and chopped
- 1 tablespoon EXTRA-VIRGIN OLIVE OIL
- ¼ tablespoon each fresh ROSEMARY, THYME, SAGE, and PARSLEY, finely chopped
- SALT and PEPPER

1. Clean the mushrooms and cut them into bite-size pieces.

2. In a sauté pan over medium heat, sauté the garlic and shallots in the olive oil until light brown, or about 2 minutes.

3. Add the mushrooms and cook, stirring constantly, for 2 minutes.

4. Add the herbs and salt and pepper to taste. Continue cooking for 2 to 3 minutes, or until the mushrooms are tender. Remove from the pan and serve immediately.

SICILIAN COUSCOUS

6 SERVINGS

You don't have to be Sicilian to love this great side dish! Sicilians use raisins in this recipe, which gives it a sweet taste.

- ½ pound uncooked COUSCOUS
- 4 tablespoons EXTRA-VIRGIN OLIVE OIL
- 1 ONION, diced
- 2 CARROTS, diced
- 2 ZUCCHINI, diced
- 2 YELLOW SQUASH, diced
- 2 pinches of SAFFRON
- 1 cup RAISINS
- SALT and PEPPER

1. Cook the couscous according to the package directions. Place in a large bowl and set aside.

2. In a large pan, heat the olive oil over medium heat. Add all the diced vegetables and the saffron and sauté for about 5 minutes, or until golden brown.

3. In a large bowl, mix the cooked couscous, vegetables, raisins, and salt and pepper to taste. Cover with plastic wrap and set aside for 5 minutes. Serve immediately.

SAFFRON RISOTTO CAKES

8 SERVINGS

You can use your leftover risotto for this recipe.

- 2 SHALLOTS, chopped
- 4 GARLIC cloves, chopped
- 4 tablespoons EXTRA-VIRGIN OLIVE OIL
- 4 cups uncooked ARBORIO RICE
- 4 cups DRY WHITE WINE
- 8 cups CHICKEN STOCK (see recipe on page 29)
- 1 cup SWEET PEAS
- 1½ cups shredded MOZZARELLA
- 2 cups grated PARMESAN CHEESE
- ½ cup BUTTER
- SALT and PEPPER
- 2 pinches of SAFFRON
- ½ cup ALL-PURPOSE FLOUR

1. In a heavy stockpot, sauté the shallots and garlic in 2 tablespoons of the olive oil over medium heat until golden brown, or 2 to 3 minutes.

2. Add the rice and white wine and cook, stirring constantly, over medium-high heat until the wine is reduced by half. Slowly add the chicken stock and cook for about 15 minutes, stirring constantly to make sure the rice does not stick to the bottom of the pan.

3. When the rice is almost cooked, add the peas, cheeses, butter, salt and pepper to taste, and saffron.

4. Cook for another 5 minutes until the rice takes on a creamy texture. Transfer to a nonstick baking sheet. Spread the rice out to a height of about ½ inch. Let it cool for 1 hour.

5. Cut out round shapes with a 3-inch-diameter cookie cutter and lightly dust them with flour. Preheat the oven to 350°F.

6. In a sauté pan over medium heat, pan-sear the risotto cakes in the remaining 2 tablespoons olive oil until they are golden brown. Place the cakes back on the baking sheet and bake them for approximately 5 minutes, or until hot. Serve immediately.

ROASTED GARLIC MASHED POTATOES

6 SERVINGS

These mashed potatoes can accompany any dish and can be made with or without the garlic.

- 1 cup peeled GARLIC CLOVES
- 1 tablespoon EXTRA-VIRGIN OLIVE OIL
- SALT and PEPPER
- 2 pounds RED BLISS POTATOES, cut into quarters
- 7 tablespoons UNSALTED BUTTER
- 1½ cups HEAVY CREAM
- KOSHER SALT

1. Preheat the oven to 325°F. Place the garlic cloves on a baking sheet. Sprinkle with the olive oil and salt and pepper to taste, and cover with aluminum foil.

2. Roast the garlic for 1 hour. Let the garlic cool and then grind it into a paste with a food processor, blender, or spoon.

3. Place the potatoes in a saucepan full of cold water and bring to a boil over high heat. Simmer until they can easily be pierced by a fork, or about 20 minutes. Drain and set aside.

4. In another saucepan, over medium heat, melt the butter. Stir in the cream and bring the mixture to a boil.

5. Add the potatoes and garlic paste and mash the mixture to your desired texture. Season with salt and serve immediately.

LENTIL SALAD

6 SERVINGS

This salad is very good for you. It is healthful and nutritious—ideal for those who always want to look good—and it can be made a few days in advance.

- 1 pound uncooked LENTILS
- 1 CARROT, diced small
- 1 small RED ONION, diced small
- ¼ cup EXTRA-VIRGIN OLIVE OIL
- KOSHER SALT
- PEPPER

1. Bring a pot of salted water to a boil. Add the lentils and simmer for 25 minutes, or until tender. Drain the lentils, let cool, and place in a bowl.

2. Mix in the carrot, red onion, and olive oil. Add salt and pepper to taste and place on a platter.

BEAN DIP

6 SERVINGS

This bean dip is a staple at Fresco—we use it instead of butter with our homemade breads. It will last 2 or 3 days in the refrigerator.

- ½ pound uncooked CANNELLINI BEANS
- 1 cup EXTRA-VIRGIN OLIVE OIL
- 2 cloves GARLIC, minced
- 2 tablespoons chopped fresh SAGE
- SALT

1. Soak the beans in salted water overnight.

2. Rinse and add new water to cover. In a 2-quart pot, boil the beans over high heat until tender, or 20 to 25 minutes. Drain the beans and mash them with the olive oil until you achieve a creamy texture.

3. Mix in the garlic and sage. Season with salt to taste. Serve cold.

WILD MUSHROOM, CANNELLINI BEAN, AND ARTICHOKE TIMBALE

6 SERVINGS

This goes very well with lamb chops.

- ½ pound uncooked CANNELLINI BEANS
- 2 pounds BABY ARTICHOKES, cleaned and cut lengthwise into eighths
- ¼ cup chopped GARLIC
- 4 tablespoons EXTRA-VIRGIN OLIVE OIL
- 1 cup DRY WHITE WINE
- 2 pounds mixed WILD MUSHROOMS, sliced
- 1 tablespoon chopped fresh ROSEMARY
- SALT and PEPPER

1. Soak the cannellini beans in a pot of water overnight. Rinse and add new water to cover. In a large pot over medium heat, bring to a boil and cook for about 40 minutes, or until tender. Drain and cool the beans and leave at room temperature.

2. In a medium sauté pan over medium heat, sauté the baby artichokes, 1 tablespoon of the garlic, and 2 tablespoons of the olive oil for 5 minutes, or until light brown. Add the white wine and simmer for 20 minutes, or until the liquid is reduced by half.

3. In another pan over medium heat, sauté the remaining 3 tablespoons chopped garlic in the remaining 2 tablespoons olive oil for 2 minutes, or until golden brown. Add the mushrooms and sauté for 5 minutes, or until tender.

4. In a bowl, mix the artichokes, cannellini beans, and wild mushrooms. Add the rosemary and salt and pepper to taste. Serve at room temperature, or heat in a sauté pan for 1 minute before serving.

MASHED POTATOES WITH SEVRUGA CAVIAR

6 SERVINGS

We serve this very special dish on Valentine's Day. It's light, it's sexy, and it doesn't keep you in the kitchen for hours.

- 2 pounds YUKON GOLD POTATOES, peeled
- 6 tablespoons UNSALTED BUTTER
- 1 cup HEAVY CREAM
- SALT and PEPPER
- ½ cup MASCARPONE CHEESE
- 1 tablespoon SEVRUGA CAVIAR
- 2 tablespoons chopped fresh CHIVES

1. In a pot, cover the potatoes with water and cook over high heat until they are soft all the way through, or about 20 minutes.

2. In a separate pot over medium heat, melt the butter with the heavy cream.

3. Add the hot potatoes to the butter and cream and smash until you get a lumpy consistency. Add salt and pepper to taste.

4. Place the potatoes on a platter, top with the mascarpone and caviar, and garnish with the fresh chives. Serve immediately.

MUSHROOM RISOTTO CAKES

6 SERVINGS

This dish oozes with flavor. It's rich, creamy, and will complement any meat or fish.

- 4 tablespoons EXTRA-VIRGIN OLIVE OIL
- 2 pounds assorted WILD MUSHROOMS
- 1 ONION, chopped
- ½ tablespoon chopped GARLIC
- 3 cups uncooked ARBORIO RICE
- 4 cups CHICKEN STOCK
- 2 cups DRY WHITE WINE
- 1 cup chopped SUN-DRIED TOMATOES
- ½ cup chopped fresh PARSLEY
- ½ cup chopped fresh BASIL
- 1 cup BUTTER
- 1 cup grated PARMESAN CHEESE
- ½ pound MOZZARELLA CHEESE, diced
- SALT and PEPPER

1. In a sauté pan, heat 2 tablespoons of the olive oil over medium heat. Sauté the mushrooms and onion for 3 minutes, or until softened. Set aside and let cool.

2. In a large pot over medium heat, simmer the garlic in the remaining 2 tablespoons olive oil until it is golden brown, or about 2 minutes. Increase the heat to medium-high, stirring constantly, add the rice, chicken stock, and white wine and cook for 15 minutes, or until the liquid is absorbed and the texture is creamy. Add the mushrooms, sun-dried tomatoes, parsley, basil, butter, Parmesan, and mozzarella and cook for another 5 minutes, or until the rice is al dente. Add salt and pepper to taste.

3. Rub a baking sheet with butter. Turn the risotto onto the sheet, spread out to a height of about ½ inch, and set aside to cool. When the risotto is cool and firm, cut it into disks with a 2½-inch round cookie cutter.

4. Right before serving, bake the risotto cakes on a baking sheet for 10 minutes in a 350°F oven.

Marion and Anthony Sr.'s wedding, 1957.

Many years ago my son John told me to sit down and relax; he would barbecue the steaks for dinner.

Elaina, Rosanna, and I waited anxiously for the food to arrive. Johnny proudly brought the steaks in, and although the aroma was good, they were a funny metallic-gold color. I asked him about it, he told me that he had marinated the steaks with the liquid he found by the grill. When I looked closely at the can, it was labeled LIGHTER FUEL.

To this day I only allow John to grill asparagus.

His winning charm and personality outshine his cooking abilities, and now he owns a very successful nightclub called Etoile.

—*Marion*

GRILLED ASPARAGUS

4 SERVINGS

This is very easy to make—and so good for you. We love serving asparagus in the summer.

1 pound ASPARAGUS, trimmed

SALT and PEPPER

3 tablespoons EXTRA-VIRGIN OLIVE OIL

1. Blanch the asparagus in boiling water, shock it in ice water, and drain. Grill it over medium heat for 2 to 3 minutes, or until light brown grill marks appear.

2. Add the salt and pepper and brush lightly with the oil. Serve immediately or at room temperature.

ROASTED WINTER VEGETABLES

4 SERVINGS

Use these vegetables, or substitute other seasonal vegetables.

- 2 CARROTS
- 2 PARSNIPS
- 4 CELERY STALKS
- 2 tablespoons EXTRA-VIRGIN OLIVE OIL
- SALT and PEPPER

1. Preheat the oven to 350°F. Cut the vegetables in half lengthwise, then slice diagonally into pieces about ¼ inch thick.

2. Place the vegetables in a roasting pan with the olive oil. Season with salt and pepper and roast for 10 to 15 minutes, or until tender.

TRICOLORE BEAN STEW

6 SERVINGS

This hearty and nourishing side dish could also be used as a warm salad.

- ½ pound uncooked CRANBERRY BEANS
- ½ pound uncooked BLACK BEANS
- ½ pound uncooked CANNELLINI BEANS
- ½ cup fresh ROSEMARY
- 1 ONION, chopped
- 1½ tablespoons chopped GARLIC
- 2 tablespoons EXTRA-VIRGIN OLIVE OIL
- ½ cup chopped fresh PARSLEY
- 1 cup grated PARMESAN CHEESE
- SALT and PEPPER

1. Soak all the beans in water overnight. Drain and rinse. Transfer the beans to a large pot and add the rosemary and enough water to cover the beans. Bring to a boil over high heat and then lower the heat to medium and simmer 25 to 30 minutes, or until the beans are tender. Drain and cool.

2. In a sauté pan over medium heat, sauté the onion and garlic in the olive oil until golden brown, or 2 to 3 minutes. Add the beans and parsley and sauté for 5 minutes.

3. While the beans are still hot, toss with the Parmesan cheese. Add salt and pepper to taste.

SAUTÉED STRING BEANS

4 SERVINGS

These string beans are easy to make—and they taste great.

- 1 pound STRING BEANS
- 2 tablespoons EXTRA-VIRGIN OLIVE OIL
- 1 tablespoon chopped GARLIC
- SALT and PEPPER

1. Clean the string beans and cut off their tops and bottoms. Blanch in boiling salted water for 2 minutes, then immediately shock in ice water to cool. Drain and set aside.

2. In a saucepan, heat the olive oil over medium heat and sauté the garlic about 2 minutes, or until golden.

3. Toss in the string beans and cook for 2 to 3 minutes, or until heated through. Add salt and pepper to taste. Serve hot.

ROASTED POTATOES

6 SERVINGS

- 2 pounds very small NEW POTATOES
- 2 tablespoons OLIVE OIL
- 6 GARLIC cloves, peeled
- 2 large sprigs ROSEMARY, leaves only
- SALT and PEPPER

1. Preheat the oven to 425°F. Toss the potatoes, olive oil, garlic, and rosemary in a bowl. Sprinkle with salt and pepper to taste.

2. Place on a baking sheet and roast for 12 to 15 minutes, or until the potatoes are soft.

POLENTA CAKES

6 SERVINGS

Polenta is a staple of Italian cooking, and everyone loves it.

- 8 cups CHICKEN STOCK (see recipe on page 29)
- 2 cups instant POLENTA
- 1½ cups grated PARMESAN CHEESE
- 2 tablespoons chopped fresh PARSLEY
- 2 teaspoons SALT

1. Bring the chicken stock to a boil over medium heat. Slowly sprinkle the polenta into the boiling liquid and stir constantly for 8 minutes over medium heat, or until the polenta thickens.

2. Add 1 cup of the cheese, the parsley, and the salt and mix well over low heat.

3. Pour the polenta into a buttered baking pan and level the top. Cool thoroughly.

4. Preheat the oven to 450°F. Cut into 2-inch squares and sprinkle generously with the remaining ½ cup Parmesan cheese. Bake until the cheese melts and the polenta cakes are golden brown, or about 5 minutes.

six

DESSERTS

THESE DESSERTS ARE GREAT FOR ENTERTAINING AT HOME. THERE ARE SEVERAL THAT ARE PERFECT FOR HOLIDAYS OR SPECIAL OCCASIONS, BUT MOST OF THEM ARE EASY FOR THE HOME CHEF TO PREPARE.

STRUFFOLI

6 SERVINGS

Danger! These little honey balls are highly addictive. We serve them at Christmas every year. When I prepare the Struffoli during the holidays, my grandchildren enjoy watching me decorate this Christmas treat. —Marion

- 12 EGGS
- Pinch of SALT
- ½ cup RYE WHISKEY
- 6 cups ALL-PURPOSE FLOUR
- CANOLA OIL
- 4 cups HONEY
- Juice of 1 LEMON
- 1 cup finely chopped WALNUTS

1. In a medium bowl, beat the eggs, salt, and rye with a wooden spoon until blended.

2. Pour the flour onto a pastry board and make a well in the center. Pour in the egg mixture and knead the dough until all the egg mixture is absorbed.

3. Cover the dough and let stand for 20 minutes.

4. In a large pot, heat 3 inches of canola oil to 350°F. Break off a palm-size piece of the dough and, using your hands, roll into a cylinder about the thickness of a pencil. Cut off ½-inch pieces and deep-fry in the hot oil until golden brown. Repeat with the remaining dough. Set aside on paper towels to drain the oil.

5. When all the pieces are fried, combine the honey, lemon juice, and chopped walnuts in a large pot. Set over medium heat and heat until the mixture boils.

6. Pour the melted honey mixture over the Struffoli and stir to coat. Pile high on a platter and serve.

PUMPKIN CHOCOLATE TIRAMISÙ

12 SERVINGS

This is a twist on traditional tiramisù. The chocolate and pumpkin add richness to an already sinful dessert. It's a big hit at Thanksgiving. My cousin, Jan Lacqua, uses this recipe when she entertains; it's fast and easy to make.

- 4 EGG YOLKS (see note on page 93)
- 1¼ cups SUGAR
- 2 cups PUMPKIN PUREE
- 2 cups MASCARPONE (18 ounces)
- 1½ cups HEAVY CREAM
- 4 sheets GELATIN
- ¼ cup BRANDY
- 2 cups ESPRESSO
- 1 10-inch layer CHOCOLATE CAKE

1. In the bowl of an electric mixer, whip the egg yolks on high speed with ¾ cup of the sugar until the mixture is pale yellow and tripled in volume.

2. Add the pumpkin and mascarpone, and whip again until light, or about 2 minutes on high speed.

3. Transfer the pumpkin mixture to a large mixing bowl. Put the cream and ¼ cup of the sugar into the bowl of the machine. Whip the cream until stiff peaks form, then fold the cream into the pumpkin mixture.

4. Soak the gelatin sheets in cold water. Remove from the water and squeeze out the excess water. Cover with the brandy in a small saucepan and heat over a low flame just until the gelatin melts.

5. Fold a small amount of the pumpkin-cream mixture into the gelatin to temper it, then mix all the gelatin into the cream.

6. Dissolve the remaining ¼ cup sugar in the espresso. Divide the cake layer in half horizontally, place one layer on a serving plate, and soak that layer with half of the espresso.

7. Pour half of the cream mixture on top of the espresso-soaked layer. Place the second cake layer on top of the cream. Soak that layer with the remaining espresso and top it with the rest of the cream. Wrap in plastic wrap and refrigerate at least overnight.

RASPBERRY-MASCARPONE TART

12 SERVINGS

Simple . . . elegant . . . perfect!

FOR THE PASTRY DOUGH

- 1 cup ALL-PURPOSE FLOUR
- 2 tablespoons CAKE FLOUR
- ¼ teaspoon SALT
- ⅛ teaspoon BAKING POWDER
- ½ cup cold BUTTER
- 3 to 4 tablespoons ICE WATER

FOR THE FILLING

- 2 cups MASCARPONE (18 ounces)
- ⅓ cup SUGAR
- 1 teaspoon VANILLA EXTRACT
- 4 to 6 half-pints fresh RASPBERRIES

1. *To make the pastry dough:* Combine the flours, salt, and baking powder in the bowl of an electric mixer with a paddle attachment. Mix on the lowest speed until the ingredients are combined, or about 30 seconds.

2. Cut the butter into eight to ten pieces and add it to the dry ingredients. Mix on the lowest speed until the butter is cut in and the mixture resembles coarse sand.

3. With the mixer running on the lowest speed, pour in the water in a thin stream. Continue mixing until the dough masses around the paddle, or 10 to 15 seconds. Scrape the dough from the paddle and the bowl, wrap in plastic, and refrigerate for at least 2 hours.

4. When the dough is well chilled, roll to a thickness of ⅛ inch on a lightly floured surface. Lay the dough into a 10-inch tart pan. Freeze the tart for 1 hour to keep the dough from shrinking while baking.

5. Preheat the oven to 350°F. Remove the tart from the freezer, cover it with foil (shiny side down), and fill it with dried beans. Bake for 20 minutes, then remove foil and beans and bake for another 10 minutes, or until light golden brown. Cool.

6. *To make the filling:* Combine the mascarpone, sugar, and vanilla. Spread evenly over the bottom of the tart shell. Top with the fresh raspberries and serve.

CHOCOLATE MASCARPONE CREAM PIE

8 SERVINGS

We made this dessert for Joan Hamburg, a very popular personality on WOR Radio in New York. Joan has been a customer at Fresco since we opened. Recently, Joan had a celebration party here and chose Chocolate Mascarpone Cream Pie for her dessert. She loved it so much that she mentioned it during her broadcast. She received so many phone calls for the recipe that she told all of her listeners to send a self-addressed and stamped envelope to Fresco and we would send them the recipe. Within a week, we received well over 2,000 requests for the Chocolate Mascarpone Cream Pie. I had to hire an extra person to help with the mail. Joan's listeners are loyal and devoted! —Rosanna

FOR THE GRAHAM CRACKER CRUST

- 1½ cups GRAHAM CRACKER CRUMBS
- ½ cup SUGAR
- ½ cup ALL-PURPOSE FLOUR
- 1½ cups BUTTER, melted

FOR THE CHOCOLATE FILLING

- 1 cup SUGAR
- ¼ cup CORNSTARCH
- ¼ teaspoon SALT
- 3 cups WHOLE MILK
- 3 EGG YOLKS, slightly beaten
- 2 tablespoons BUTTER
- 2 teaspoons VANILLA EXTRACT
- ¼ cup finely chopped unsweetened CHOCOLATE

WHIPPED TOPPING

- 2 cups MASCARPONE (18 ounces)
- 2 cups HEAVY CREAM
- ¼ cup SUGAR
- 1 teaspoon VANILLA EXTRACT

1. *To make the graham cracker crust:* Preheat the oven to 350°F. In a medium bowl, mix the ingredients for the crust together until blended. Press into the bottom and sides of a 9-inch pie pan to a thickness of about ¼ inch (you'll have some left over). Bake for 12 minutes, or until golden brown. Let cool.

2. *To make the chocolate filling:* In a medium saucepan, combine the sugar, cornstarch, and salt. Stir in the milk, blending well. Cook over medium heat, stirring constantly, until the mixture boils and thickens, or about 2 minutes. Remove from the heat.

3. Blend a small amount of the hot mixture into the egg yolks to temper them. Pour the egg yolks into the saucepan, blending thoroughly.

4. Heat the mixture over high heat, stirring constantly, until it just begins to bubble, or about 3 minutes. Remove from the heat and stir in the butter, vanilla, and chocolate. Stir until the chocolate melts completely.

5. Pour the mixture into the baked pie shell and refrigerate, uncovered, for at least 1 hour.

6. *To make the whipped topping:* In a large bowl, combine all the topping ingredients and whip until stiff. Spread over the filling and return the pie to the refrigerator for at least 2 more hours.

FRESH BERRIES WITH ZABAGLIONE

6 SERVINGS

A classic Italian dessert—and possibly one of the easiest to make. It's a great dessert for the summer season.

- 3 EGG YOLKS
- ¼ cup SUGAR
- ¼ cup MARSALA WINE (or CHAMPAGNE, ORANGE JUICE, or virtually any drink)
- 4½ cups fresh BERRIES (STRAWBERRIES, RASPBERRIES, BLUEBERRIES, or your favorite—or a mixture)

1. Combine the egg yolks, sugar, and wine in the top of a double boiler. Whisk briskly for 2 to 3 minutes, or until thickened.

2. Spoon the liquid over the fresh berries and serve.

ARBORIO RICE PUDDING

6 SERVINGS

This is the ultimate comfort food. When you're feeling bad, it's a real pick-me-up!

- 1 quart plus 1 cup HEAVY CREAM
- 2 cups WHOLE MILK
- ¾ cup ARBORIO RICE
- 3 whole EGGS
- 5 EGG YOLKS
- 1 cup SUGAR
- 1 tablespoon VANILLA EXTRACT
- 1½ teaspoons ground CINNAMON
- 2 teaspoons ORANGE FLOWER WATER (available in specialty food stores)
- 1 cup chopped DATES

1. Combine 1 quart of the cream, the milk, and the rice in a medium saucepan. Bring to a boil over high heat, stirring constantly. Cover and simmer over low heat for 20 minutes, or until creamy.

2. In a medium bowl, whisk together the eggs, egg yolks, sugar, vanilla, cinnamon, and orange flower water. Set aside.

3. Add a small amount of the hot liquid into the egg mixture, mix well, and add the rest. Stir in the remaining 1 cup cream and the chopped dates.

4. Preheat the oven to 350°F. Pour the mixture into a 4-quart casserole. Place the casserole in a larger pan and put the pan in the oven. Pour enough hot water into the pan to fill it halfway. Bake the pudding for 40 to 45 minutes, or until set.

A few days after September 11, 2001, Fred Wilpon, president and chief executive officer of the New York Mets, came into Fresco for dinner. At that time, restaurants in New York were empty and business was at an all-time low.

When Fred was eating his dessert, he noticed that the restaurant was not busy. He wondered how my wonderful staff was surviving during this terrible time. I assured him that Fresco would survive even if I had to pay my staff extra to remain open for our customers.

At that point, Fred emptied his pockets and left enough money for every waiter in the restaurant. That evening every staff member went home with a full day's pay.

Thank you, Mr. Wilpon! Your generosity and kindness will always be remembered!

—Marion

LOVE TRIFLE

12 SERVINGS

This recipe is a little complicated, but it's guaranteed to bring a little love into your life. We serve it on Valentine's Day, as it makes an unbelievable presentation.

FOR THE FILLING

- 8 EGG YOLKS
- 1 cup SUGAR
- 2 teaspoons VANILLA EXTRACT
- 4 cups MASCARPONE (or 2 18-ounce containers)
- 3½ cups HEAVY CREAM
- 2 sheets GELATIN
- 1 cup chopped semisweet CHOCOLATE

FOR THE VANILLA SPONGE CAKE

- 1½ cups ALL-PURPOSE FLOUR
- 1½ cups CORNSTARCH
- 12 EGGS
- 1¼ cups SUGAR
- 4 teaspoons VANILLA EXTRACT

FOR THE ASSEMBLY

- 4 half-pints fresh RASPBERRIES
- 3 cups WHIPPED CREAM
- 1 cup CHOCOLATE CURLS

1. *To make the filling:* Combine the egg yolks, ¾ cup of the sugar, and the vanilla in the top of a double boiler. Cook, whisking constantly and vigorously, until the mixture has turned pale yellow and thickened, or 5 to 7 minutes.

2. Transfer the mixture to the bowl of an electric mixer and whip on high until cool. Add the mascarpone and whip for 1 minute more. Add 3 cups of the cream and the remaining ¼ cup sugar, and whip to soft peaks.

3. Soften the gelatin in cold water. Squeeze any excess water from the gelatin and melt it in a small saucepan over low heat. Fold a small amount of the cream mixture into the gelatin and fold that back into the rest of the cream. Divide the cream in half.

4. In a double boiler over low heat, melt the chocolate with the remaining ½ cup cream. Blend the chocolate mixture into half of the cream mixture. Set the chocolate-cream mixture aside.

5. *To make the vanilla sponge cake:* Sift together the flour and cornstarch. In a large bowl, whip the eggs, sugar, and vanilla until tripled in volume. Fold in the flour-cornstarch mixture.

6. Preheat the oven to 350°F. Grease and flour two 9-inch cake pans. Divide the batter between the pans. Bake for 35 to 40 minutes, or until the cakes spring back lightly when touched. When the cakes are cool, slice each into 2 layers.

7. *To assemble:* Place 1 layer of the cake in a straight-sided glass trifle bowl, cover with 1 cup of the raspberries. Spread ¼ of the vanilla cream over the raspberries. Spread ¼ of the chocolate cream over the vanilla cream. Repeat with the remaining cake layers, raspberries, and cream. Top with the whipped cream, raspberries, and chocolate curls.

I WANT YOU
TO SAVE N.Y.

CHOCOLATE-WALNUT BROWNIES

12 BROWNIES

This brownie, topped with ice cream and fudge sauce, is our biggest-selling dessert at Fresco. It's a great treat for the kids, and they love baking it themselves.

- 1¼ cups finely chopped UNSWEETENED CHOCOLATE (about 10 ounces)
- 2 cups BUTTER
- 6 EGGS
- 3 cups SUGAR
- 1 cup ALL-PURPOSE FLOUR
- 1 tablespoon BAKING POWDER
- 1½ cups SEMISWEET CHOCOLATE CHIPS
- 1½ cups chopped WALNUTS

1. In the top of a double boiler, melt the chopped chocolate and butter. Set aside. Preheat the oven to 350°F and grease and flour a 9- by 13-inch baking pan.

2. In a large bowl, whip the eggs and sugar together until pale yellow and tripled in volume. Fold in the flour and baking powder, then the melted chocolate, and then the chocolate chips and walnuts.

3. Pour the batter into the baking pan and bake for 30 minutes (it won't look done, but it is). Cut into squares.

CHOCOLATE CUPCAKES

12 CUPCAKES

This is a fun treat to make with your children. Top the cupcakes with your favorite frosting. My youngest grandchild, Bianca, is as pretty as a cupcake, and she likes to eat them, too! —Marion

- 2 cups BUTTER
- 2¾ cups SUGAR
- 6 EGGS
- 4 teaspoons VANILLA EXTRACT
- 3⅔ cups sifted CAKE FLOUR
- 2 tablespoons BAKING POWDER
- ¾ cup COCOA POWDER
- 1 cup boiling WATER

1. Preheat the oven to 350°F. Put paper cupcake liners into a 12-muffin pan. In a large bowl, cream the butter and sugar until light and fluffy. Add the eggs, one at a time, scraping down the sides of the bowl. Add the vanilla extract.

2. Fold in the flour and the baking powder. Whisk together the cocoa powder and water and mix into the batter.

3. Fill the paper cups two-thirds full and bake for 25 to 30 minutes, or until a toothpick inserted into the center of a cupcake comes out clean or the top springs back when lightly touched.

MEYER LEMON PUDDING CAKES

6 CAKES

Meyer lemons are a cross between a regular lemon and a mandarin orange. The complex flavor and aroma hint of sweet lime, lemon, and mandarin. If you can't find them, you can still use any variety of lemon.

- 2 tablespoons UNSALTED BUTTER
- ⅔ cup SUGAR
- ⅛ teaspoon SALT
- 1 tablespoon MEYER LEMON ZEST
- 3 EGG YOLKS
- 3 tablespoons ALL-PURPOSE FLOUR
- ¼ cup strained fresh MEYER LEMON JUICE
- 1 cup WHOLE MILK
- 4 EGG WHITES

1. Preheat the oven to 325°F. In a large bowl, cream the butter, sugar, salt, and lemon zest. Add the egg yolks, one at a time, scraping down the sides of the bowl to incorporate thoroughly. Add the flour and mix until smooth. Gradually stir in the lemon juice, then the milk.

2. In a clean, dry bowl, whip the egg whites until they form stiff peaks. Do not overbeat.

3. Gently fold the egg whites into the batter, just until no large lumps of white remain.

4. Ladle the batter into 6 lightly buttered 6-ounce ramekins. Set the ramekins in a larger pan. Place the pan in the oven and pour enough hot water into the pan to reach halfway up the sides of the ramekins. Bake for 30 to 40 minutes, or until a knife inserted into the center of the cakes comes out clean.

5. Let the cakes stand for 10 minutes in the water bath. Serve warm, cold, or at room temperature.

BITTERSWEET CHOCOLATE PUDDING CAKE

10 SERVINGS

This is a chocoholic's dream!

Every year my husband, Anthony, and I celebrate New Year's Eve with some friends and family at Fresco. We always end our night of dancing with this Chocolate Pudding Cake. Howard Golden (the best borough president Brooklyn ever had) and his wife, Aileen, Pat and Herb Frumkes, Fred and Judy Sullivan, and Anthony and Jacqueline Di Falco always join us for our annual celebration.

We have been friends for years. We care for one another and value our friendship. —Marion

FOR THE CHOCOLATE PUDDING CAKE

- 1¾ cups ALL-PURPOSE FLOUR
- ¼ teaspoon SALT
- 1 teaspoon BAKING SODA
- ½ cup plus 2 tablespoons unsweetened COCOA POWDER
- 1 cup BUTTER
- 1¾ cups firmly packed LIGHT BROWN SUGAR
- 4 EGGS
- 1 teaspoon VANILLA EXTRACT
- ¾ cup HOT WATER

FOR THE BUTTERSCOTCH SAUCE

- 2 cups firmly packed LIGHT BROWN SUGAR
- 1 cup BUTTER
- 1 cup HEAVY CREAM
- 3 tablespoons LIGHT CORN SYRUP

1. *To make the chocolate pudding cake:* Sift together the flour, salt, baking powder, and ½ cup of the cocoa powder.

2. In a large bowl, beat the butter and 1 cup of the brown sugar at medium speed until light. Add the eggs, one at a time, beating well after each addition. Beat in the vanilla. Stir in the flour mixture.

3. Preheat the oven to 350°F. Lightly grease a 2-quart baking dish. Spoon the batter into the dish.

4. In a small bowl, mix together the remaining ¾ cup brown sugar and 2 tablespoons cocoa powder and the hot water. Pour the liquid over the batter and place the baking dish into a larger pan. Place the pan in the oven and pour enough hot water into the pan to reach halfway up the sides of the baking dish.

5. Bake for 40 to 45 minutes, or until the pudding is barely set and has begun to pull away from the sides of the baking dish.

6. *To make the butterscotch sauce:* Combine all the ingredients in a medium saucepan, bring to a boil, and remove from the heat. Serve the pudding warm with the warm butterscotch sauce.

RICOTTA CHEESECAKE

12 SERVINGS

This combination of cream cheese and ricotta cheese produces outstanding results.

FOR THE GRAHAM CRACKER CRUST

- 1 cup GRAHAM CRACKER CRUMBS
- ¼ cup ALL-PURPOSE FLOUR
- 3 tablespoons SUGAR
- ½ cup BUTTER, melted

FOR THE RICOTTA FILLING

- 1 pound CREAM CHEESE
- 1½ pounds WHOLE MILK RICOTTA CHEESE (preferably fresh—available in Italian markets and specialty food stores)
- 6 EGGS
- 1¼ cups SUGAR
- 1 tablespoon VANILLA EXTRACT

1. *To make the graham cracker crust:* Preheat the oven to 350°F. In a medium bowl, mix all of the ingredients until blended. Line the bottom of a 10-inch springform pan with parchment or waxed paper. Tightly cover the outside of the pan with foil (it has to be watertight). Press the crumb mixture into the pan evenly, covering the bottom. Bake for 15 minutes, or until golden brown. Remove from the oven and reduce the heat to 325°F.

2. *To make the ricotta filling:* In a food processor or blender, puree the 2 cheeses together until smooth. Transfer to a mixing bowl, add the eggs, sugar, and vanilla, and whisk until well blended.

3. Pour the mixture into the crust and place that pan into a larger pan. Pour enough water into the larger pan to reach halfway up the sides of the springform pan.

4. Bake for 2 hours. At the end of this time, shut off the oven, open the oven door slightly, and allow the cheesecake to cool in the oven for at least an hour. Remove from the oven and let cool to room temperature. Refrigerate at least overnight.

5. To remove the cheesecake from the pan, run a hot, wet knife around the edge of the cake and remove the collar of the pan. Invert the cake onto a plate and remove the springform bottom and parchment paper. Flip the cake back over onto a serving plate and cut with a hot, wet knife. Serve with fresh berries.

SGROPPINO FLOAT

1 SERVING

In 1992, my family and I spent a few weeks on the Lido in Venice. We shopped, cooked, dined, and had a wonderful time. We felt like true Venetians. We ate at small restaurants, where the food was simple yet full of different flavors.

Every evening I noticed that people were ordering this wonderful dessert drink . . . It took us a day to learn how to pronounce it (sgrō–pé–nō). Once we got it right, we ordered it every night.

Sgroppino Floats are on Fresco's summer menu every year.

—Anthony Jr.

1 tablespoon RASPBERRY SYRUP

2 scoops LEMON ICE CREAM

1 cup SPARKLING WINE (PROSECCO, ASTI SPUMANTE, or CHAMPAGNE) or GINGER ALE

Pour the raspberry syrup into an ice-cream-soda glass, add the ice cream, and pour in sparkling wine to fill.

ORANGE BUNDT CAKE

12 SERVINGS

This cake can keep for days and still be moist. It's the perfect cake to put on a dessert buffet. It's light and rich with flavor.

- 2 cups BUTTER, soft
- 4¼ cups SUGAR
- 4½ cups sifted CAKE FLOUR
- 2¼ teaspoons BAKING POWDER
- ½ teaspoon SALT
- ½ cup MILK
- 9 EGGS
- 1 tablespoon plus 1½ teaspoons VANILLA EXTRACT
- Zest of 3 ORANGES, minced
- 2 cups ORANGE JUICE

1. Preheat the oven to 350°F. Grease and flour a Bundt pan. Cream the butter together with 2¼ cups of the sugar. Add the flour, baking powder, and salt and mix until combined. Add the milk, eggs, vanilla, and orange zest. Pour the batter into the Bundt pan.

2. Bake for 1 hour and 15 minutes, or until a toothpick inserted into the middle of the cake comes out clean. Poke holes all over the cake with a toothpick and let it cool thoroughly.

3. Combine the orange juice and the remaining 2 cups of sugar in a small saucepan. Bring to a boil over high heat. Paint the sauce onto the cake with a pastry brush.

CHILLED MIXED BERRY SOUP

8 SERVINGS

What a refreshing way to begin or end your meal!

- 2 cups STRAWBERRIES, hulled and quartered
- 2 cups RASPBERRIES
- 2 cups BLUEBERRIES
- 2 cups BLACKBERRIES
- 2 cups RED WINE (any kind)
- 2 cups SUGAR
- 1 stick CINNAMON
- Additional fresh BERRIES for garnish

1. Combine all the ingredients, except the garnish, in a large saucepan and bring to a boil over high heat.

2. Reduce the heat to low and simmer until the alcohol evaporates and the soup is slightly thickened, or 20 to 25 minutes.

3. Chill the soup and remove the cinnamon stick. Garnish with the berries and serve with vanilla ice cream.

BRUTTI MA BUONI

4 DOZEN COOKIES

Brutti ma buoni *means "ugly but good"—and that's exactly what these cookies are!*

1 cup EGG WHITES

2 pounds POWDERED SUGAR

1 cup COCOA POWDER

2 pounds MIXED NUTS

1. Preheat the oven to 300°F. In a clean, dry bowl, whip the egg whites until they begin to foam. Gradually add the powdered sugar and whip until a stiff meringue forms.

2. Fold in the cocoa powder and nuts, drop by spoonfuls onto a greased cookie sheet. Bake for 35 minutes, or until shiny. The cookies will crisp upon cooling.

FRESCO STRAWBERRY SHORTCAKE

4 SERVINGS

A little-known Italian fact: With its sweet but sharp taste, balsamic vinegar tastes great on strawberries. Just a few drops adds a glorious flavor to your dessert.

FOR THE ALMOND SHORTBREAD

- 1½ cups whole unblanched ALMONDS
- 4½ cups ALL-PURPOSE FLOUR
- 2 cups UNSALTED BUTTER
- ½ cup GRANULATED SUGAR
- ½ cup firmly packed LIGHT BROWN SUGAR
- 9 EGG YOLKS

FOR THE BASIL SYRUP

- 1 cup WATER
- 1 cup GRANULATED SUGAR
- 1½ cups chopped fresh BASIL

FOR THE ASSEMBLY

- 3 cups STRAWBERRIES, hulled and quartered
- GRANULATED SUGAR
- ½ cup BALSAMIC VINEGAR
- ¼ cup finely chopped fresh BASIL
- 2 cups WHIPPED CREAM

1. *To make the almond shortbread:* Preheat the oven to 350°F. Spread the almonds on a baking sheet and toast for 5 to 7 minutes. Put the almonds and flour in a food processor and process until the nuts are finely ground.

2. In a large mixing bowl, cream the butter and sugars. Mix in the egg yolks one at a time, scraping down the sides of the bowl to incorporate the yolks completely. Add the nuts and mix just until combined. Wrap the dough in plastic and refrigerate for 1 hour.

3. Preheat the oven to 350°F. When the dough is well chilled, transfer to a lightly floured surface, then roll out to a thickness of ¼ inch and cut into shapes (e.g., triangles).

4. Place the shortbread on a greased or parchment-lined baking sheet and bake for 18 to 20 minutes, or until golden brown.

5. *To make the basil syrup:* In a small saucepan, bring the water and sugar to a boil. Add the basil and cook for 1 minute more. Puree in a blender until smooth. Strain through a fine mesh sieve and set aside.

6. *To assemble:* Place the strawberries in a large bowl and mix in sugar to taste (go a little heavier than you normally would). Let sit for a few minutes to allow the sugar to dissolve. Splash the berries with the balsamic vinegar.

7. Divide the strawberries among 4 plates. Drizzle each serving with basil syrup and sprinkle with finely chopped basil. Serve with the almond shortbread cookies and whipped cream.

PRALINE COOKIE ICE CREAM SANDWICHES

3 DOZEN COOKIES OR 18 ICE CREAM SANDWICHES

Recently, former president Bill Clinton and Senator Hillary Rodham Clinton celebrated their wedding anniversary with fourteen guests at Fresco. It caused a lot of excitement in the restaurant. One of the highlights of the evening was their anniversary dessert, which had to be served on two separate platters because Hillary and Bill sat opposite each other. We presented a platter of seven ice cream sandwiches for Hillary and a platter of seven ice cream sandwiches for the president, each with a candle. Hillary blew out her candle and then the captain served each guest on Hillary's side an ice cream sandwich. Bill blew out his candle but didn't share his dessert. He just ate and ate and ate . . . seven ice cream sandwiches!

The captain ran into the kitchen to make six more desserts for their guests. —Marion

½ cup EGG WHITES

1 cup firmly packed DARK BROWN SUGAR

4 cups PECAN HALVES

CINNAMON or other ICE CREAM

CHOCOLATE SAUCE (homemade or store-bought)

1. Preheat the oven to 300°F. In a large bowl, whip the egg whites until they begin to foam. Gradually add the brown sugar and whip until a stiff meringue forms. Fold in the nuts.

2. Drop the batter by the tablespoonful onto greased cookie sheets and bake for 45 minutes, or until golden brown.

3. To make an ice cream sandwich, put a scoop of the cinnamon ice cream between two of the cookies and top with chocolate sauce.

RICOTTA FRITTERS

25 TO 30 FRITTERS

Just one bite of these fritters and you'll be transported to an Italian street festival. They really take us back to the Feast of San Gennaro, which is celebrated every year in Little Italy. When we were younger, a visit to this street festival was a must.

Now we make Ricotta Fritters at Fresco! —Marion

- 4 EGGS, lightly beaten
- ¾ cup POWDERED SUGAR
- 1 pound RICOTTA CHEESE
- ½ teaspoon VANILLA EXTRACT
- ½ cup ALL-PURPOSE FLOUR
- ½ cup CAKE FLOUR
- 1 tablespoon BAKING POWDER
- Pinch of SALT
- OIL for frying
- 1 cup HONEY, warmed
- 1 cup FRUIT PRESERVES

1. In a large bowl, combine the eggs and ¼ cup of the powdered sugar. Mix in the ricotta and vanilla.

2. In another large bowl, sift together the dry ingredients. Fold them into the ricotta mixture and beat until smooth.

3. Fill a pot (or deep fryer) with oil to a depth of 3 inches and heat to 350°F.

4. Drop the dough into the hot oil by the tablespoonful. Fry the fritters a few at a time until golden brown, or about 3 minutes.

5. Remove the fritters from the oil and place on paper towels to drain. Dust with the remaining ½ cup powdered sugar, drizzle with warm honey, and serve with the fruit preserves immediately.

Marion's communion.

SOUR CREAM STREUSEL CAKE

12 SERVINGS

This is great for dunking in a big cup of coffee or a glass of milk—for breakfast or a late-night snack.

FOR THE CAKE

- 4 cups ALL-PURPOSE FLOUR
- 1 tablespoon BAKING POWDER
- 1 teaspoon BAKING SODA
- Pinch of SALT
- 1½ cups BUTTER, melted
- 1⅓ cups SUGAR
- 4 EGGS
- 1 tablespoon VANILLA EXTRACT
- 2 cups SOUR CREAM

FOR THE STREUSEL

- 1 cup firmly packed LIGHT BROWN SUGAR
- 1 cup ALL-PURPOSE FLOUR
- 2 teaspoons ground CINNAMON
- ½ cup BUTTER
- 1 teaspoon VANILLA EXTRACT
- 2¼ cups chopped PECANS

1. *To make the cake:* In a large bowl, mix the flour, baking powder, baking soda, and salt. In another bowl, mix the butter, sugar, eggs, vanilla, and sour cream. Combine the two mixtures and mix well.

2. *To make the streusel:* Mix together the sugar, flour, and cinnamon. Cut in the butter, then add the vanilla and the pecans. The mixture should be crumbly.

3. Preheat the oven to 350°F. Grease and flour a tube cake pan. Pour half the batter into the cake pan and top with half the streusel. Repeat with the remaining batter and streusel. Bake for 1 hour, or until golden brown.

Index